• CELEBRATING HOLIDAYS & FESTIVALS AROUND THE WORLD •

Carnival

Betsy Richardson

MC

MASON CREST

Mason Crest
450 Parkway Drive, Suite D Broomall, PA 19008
www.masoncrest.com

Printed in the United States of America
First printing
9 8 7 6 5 4 3 2 1

Series ISBN: 978-1-4222-4143-1
Hardcover 978-1-4222-4144-8

Library of Congress Cataloging-in-Publication Data is available on file.

Developed and Produced by Print Matters Productions, Inc. (www.printmattersinc.com)
Cover and Interior Design by Lori S Malkin Design, LLC

• CELEBRATING HOLIDAYS & FESTIVALS AROUND THE WORLD •

KEY ICONS TO LOOK FOR:

 Words to understand: These words with their easy-to-understand definitions will increase the reader's understanding of the text while building vocabulary skills.

 Sidebars: This boxed material within the main text allows readers to build knowledge, gain insights, explore possibilities, and broaden their perspectives by weaving together additional information to provide realistic and holistic perspectives.

 Educational Videos: Readers can view videos by scanning our QR codes, providing them with additional educational content to supplement the text. Examples include news coverage, moments in history, speeches, iconic sports moments and much more!

 Text-dependent Questions: These questions send the reader back to the text for more careful attention to the evidence presented there.

 Research projects: Readers are pointed toward areas of further inquiry connected to each chapter. Suggestions are provided for projects that encourage deeper research and analysis.

 Series glossary of key terms: This back-of-the book glossary contains terminology used throughout this series. Words found here increase the reader's ability to read and comprehend higher-level books and articles in this field.

CONTENTS

INTRODUCTION

Celebrating Holidays & Festivals Around the World

Holidays mark time. They occupy a space outside of ordinary events and give shape and meaning to our everyday existence. They also remind us of the passage of time as we reflect on Christmases, Passovers, or Ramadans past. Throughout human history, nations and peoples have marked their calendars with special days to celebrate, commemorate, and memorialize. We set aside times to reflect on the past and future, to rest and renew physically and spiritually, and to simply have fun.

In English we call these extraordinary moments "holidays," a contraction of the term "holy day." Sometimes holidays are truly holy days–the Sabbath, Easter, or Eid al-Fitr, for example–but they can also be nonreligious occasions that serve political purposes, address the social needs of communities and individuals, or focus on regional customs and games.

This series explores the meanings and celebrations of holidays across religions and cultures around the world. It groups the holidays into volumes according to theme (such as *Lent, Yom Kippur & Days of Repentance*; *Thanksgiving & Other Festivals of the Harvest*; *Independence Days*; *Easter, Passover & Festivals of Hope*; *Ringing in the Western & Chinese New Year*; *Marking the Religious New Year*; *Carnival*; *Ramadan*; and *Halloween & Remembrances of the Dead*) or by their common human experience due to their closeness on the calendar (such as *Christmas & Hanukkah*). Each volume introduces readers to the origins, history, and common practices associated with the holidays before embarking on a worldwide tour that shows the regional variations and distinctive celebrations within specific countries. The reader will learn how these holidays started, what they mean to the people who celebrate them, and how different cultures celebrate them.

▲ A Carnival dancer in full costume at the start of the celebrations in Santa Catarina, Brazil.

These volumes have an international focus, and thus readers will be able to learn about diversity both at home and throughout the world. We can learn a great deal about a people or nation by the holidays they celebrate. We can also learn from holidays how cultures and religions have interacted and mingled over time. We see in celebrations not just the past through tradition, but the principles and traits that people embrace and value today.

The Celebrating Holidays & Festivals Around the World series surveys this rich and varied festive terrain. Its 10 volumes show the distinct ways that people all over the world infuse ordinary life with meaning, purpose, or joy. The series cannot be all-inclusive or the last word on so vast a subject, but it offers a vital first step for those eager to learn more about the diverse, fascinating, and vibrant cultures of the world, through the festivities that give expression, order, and meaning to their lives.

Carnival

Of all the holidays celebrated across the modern world, Carnival might be the most boisterous, and possibly the most fun. In the Christian religion, from Eastern Europe to the Americas, Carnival offers revelers an opportunity to celebrate the pleasures of life. It is usually observed during a Carnival season that begins in the weeks before Lent, the traditional Christian fast before Easter. This festival is primarily a Roman Catholic tradition and, to a lesser degree, it is observed in Christian Orthodox communities as well. Carnival is known for its exuberance, color, creativity, and culture. In many countries people celebrate the holiday with lavish parades, jubilant dancing, and nonstop music. Parade participants create elaborate floats and march through the streets in glittering, colorful costumes. Musical groups face off in marathon competitions, and young men and women dress their best in the hope of being named the Carnival king and queen, ceremonial dignitaries who may lead a parade or reign over a ball.

▲ A samba school member dances in a parade in Rio de Janeiro, Brazil.

Origins of Carnival

■ Pagan Roots

There are many theories about the origins of Carnival. The people of Europe celebrated festivals similar to today's Carnival long before the spread of Christianity. Many of these festivals were deeply rooted in pagan tradition. (In this context "pagan" refers to people who do not believe in one god but many gods who are closely connected to nature and the natural world.)

CELEBRATING DIONYSUS AND BACCHUS

The ancient Greeks honored Dionysus, the god of wine, pleasure, fertility, and drama, with a raucous festival called The Great Dionysias. The Great Dionysias was celebrated each year in the spring (March or April) in the city of Athens. The festival consisted of five or six days of food, drink, music, and theatrical events. Many Greek comedies and

WORDS TO UNDERSTAND

Abstinence: Denying oneself a pleasure, often for religious reasons.
Rambunctious: Disorderly, unruly, wild.
Somber: Serious, reserved, grave.

◀ Statues of Bacchus, the Roman god of wine and pleasure, are common to see in places like Florence, Italy.

tragedies also debuted at this festival as an act of worship of Dionysus who was believed to be present at the performances. The ancient Romans continued the tradition in the form of Bacchanalia, a festival named for Bacchus, the Roman god of wine and pleasure. Originally, Bacchanalia was celebrated for three days during the early spring to mark the beginning of a new planting season, and only women celebrated it. The festivities were marked by large amounts of wine consumption, song, and dance. Over time men were included in the celebration and soon the frequency of the festivals increased to up to five times a month. People began celebrating in seasons other than the spring. Eventually Bacchanalia celebrations became so rowdy that the Roman Senate had to outlaw them. Today the word *bacchanalia* has come to mean any boisterous celebration marked by overindulgence in food or drink.

SATURNALIA

The Romans also celebrated the festival of Saturnalia every year in honor of the god of agriculture, Saturn. Many of the traditions of Saturnalia were incorporated over time into both Christmas and Carnival, including the exchange of gifts and the ritual of a triumphal procession through the city streets. In Rome, where winters were not as harsh as those in the far North, Saturnalia celebrations began in the week leading up to the winter solstice (around December 16) and continued for a full month, with much eating, drinking, and mischief. Practices normally forbidden in Roman society, such as public gambling, were permitted during Saturnalia. The celebration intentionally turned Roman society hierarchies upside-down. For a month slaves were masters (slavery was common in the Roman Empire) and peasants controlled the city. Hedonism (the philosophy that the greatest good lies in the pursuit of pleasure) characterized the entire festival.

LUPERCALIA

Another ancient Roman festival that may have contributed to Carnival was Lupercalia, a festival held on February 15 celebrating the Roman god Lupercus, a deity who guarded the shepherds and their flocks protecting them from wolves. He is often associated with Faunus, the Roman god of fertility and the woodlands. Faunus was believed to be the grandson of Saturn. (Most people are familiar with his Greek counterpart, Pan, a god who is usually pictured as having the legs and horns of a goat and playing a panpipe.) Faunus was associated with merriment and revelry; and noise, high spirits, and lack of restraint characterized festivals held in his honor. Special priests called Luperci oversaw the festival of Lupercalia. They offered sacrifices of two goats and a dog to

▲ A merrymaker embraces the spirit of Carnival in a parade at the Barranquilla Carnival in Colombia.

Lupercus; in return the god was expected to protect the flocks for the coming year. During the feast of Lupercalia, offerings were also made to Juno, the Roman goddess of women and marriage. After the sacrifices the priests would run around waving strips of goatskin and strike anyone who got in their way, especially women. Many women wanted to be struck with the goatskin because it was thought to bring fertility.

Although the precise origin of Lupercalia is unknown, the fact that it took place on the Palatine Hill suggests it dates back to the early days of Rome, when the cultural life of the city revolved around that site. (Palatine Hill is the centermost of the seven hills of ancient Rome where the homes of the emperors were located.) Whatever its origin, the holiday attained such popularity that it was celebrated from ancient times until 494 C.E., when it was incorporated into Christianity.

■ Carnival Becomes Christian

Often the early Roman Catholic Church turned festivals that were already celebrated by the local people into religious holidays, partly in an effort to win converts. In 494 C.E. the Catholic Church under Pope Gelasius I adapted Lupercalia into the Feast of the Purification of the Blessed Virgin Mary, a commemoration of the day Mary–after observing the traditional 40-day waiting period of purification after the birth of Jesus–presented her son to God at the Temple of Jerusalem. (Most historians believe Jesus was a real person who grew up in Nazareth, a town in northern Israel. However, the foundation of Christianity lies in the belief that Jesus was not just a person but also the son of God–a divine being in human form.) The Feast of the Purification, more commonly known as Candlemas, is celebrated on February 2 by members of several Christian faiths, most notably Roman Catholics and some Orthodox Christians.

Historians believe that the wild exuberance of Bacchanalia, Saturnalia, and Lupercalia was carried over to the Carnival of today. As time passed, the Carnivals grew famous and spread rapidly across the Catholic countries of Europe. While the general public also participates in the fun during Carnival, the holiday has a special meaning to religious individuals: immediately following the festivities, the **somber** season of Lent begins. Lent is the 40-day period leading up to Easter Sunday, the day Christians believe Jesus Christ rose from the dead after having been crucified on Good Friday. During Lent, Catholics, some Protestants, and Orthodox Christians are expected to practice extreme piety, or goodness; penance, a form of suffering one puts upon him- or herself to make up for previous misdeeds; and **abstinence**, or self-restraint. They are also expected

ORTHODOX CHRISTIANS

Orthodox Christians separated from the Catholic Church in 1054 when they refused to acknowledge the rule of the Catholic Church's spiritual leader, Pope Leo IX. Though the Roman Catholic Church follows the Gregorian calendar and the several churches associated with the Eastern Orthodox Church follow the Julian calendar, Carnival is usually celebrated roughly around the same time by both, depending on the date of Easter. Some years the celebration may be as much as a month apart; other years it may fall on the same day.

to refrain from eating meat on certain days. Although there are numerous theories pertaining to the origins of the name *Carnival*, the most widely accepted one states that the name is derived from the Italian *carnevale* or *carnovale*, which literally translates to "to remove meat." The name might also have originated from the Latin words *caro*, or *carne*, meaning "flesh" or "meat" and *vale*, meaning "farewell," thus "Farewell to meat." With so much seriousness ahead, people revel in the joyful and **rambunctious** atmosphere of Carnival by indulging in these foods that will soon be off-limits in the Lenten season.

PROTESTANTS

Protestants are Christians who separated from the Catholic Church in 1517 under the leadership of German theologian Martin Luther. Luther advocated simplifying the structure, culture, and worship services and rites of Christianity.

▲ Marchers in costume parade through the streets of Basel, Switzerland, during Carnival.

■ The Spread of Carnival

Although Carnival originated in Europe, it has spread to many countries throughout the world. When Europeans began to explore and colonize the Americas, they brought their cultures, religions, and holidays with them. These European traditions began to mix with those of the indigenous, or native, peoples. As a result, each Carnival celebration reflects a rich blend of historical and cultural elements. Today Carnival gatherings in the Caribbean, Central America, South America, North America, and even Africa reveal not only the influence of the European colonizers but also the culture of the people who lived in these regions before, during, and after colonization.

Watch footage from the parades of Patras Carnival in Greece.

▲ Revelers wear handmade papier-mâché masks like these during Carnival celebrations in Haiti.

TEXT-DEPENDENT QUESTIONS

1: Who is Dionysius?

2: Name two ways the Romans celebrated Saturnalia.

3: What feast is celebrated on February 2 by members of several Christian faiths?

RESEARCH PROJECTS

1: Research one of the Greek gods who had festivals in their honor. Some examples are Apollo, Athena, and Posedion. Write a brief report summarizing what the god was known for, how the Greek people revered him or her, and some of their festival celebrations.

2: Select two countries where Carnival is celebrated. Research the unique ways that each country celebrates Carnival, the different names it might have for the celebration, and other facts. Write a brief report comparing and contrasting the two Carnival celebrations.

Celebrating Carnival

Most, if not all, Carnival festivities share a common feeling and general purpose: to celebrate life. Through music and dancing, parades and balls, food and drink, Carnival is a time to rejoice and have fun. It is also a time to add an element of fantasy to the day-to-day reality of a culture or people. This is done through such activities as **masquerades**, or gatherings in which participants dress in elaborate costumes and masks so as to blur the lines between dream and reality. Bringing a sense of exuberance while accompanied by horses and **papier-mâché** floats, masqueraders will often parade through the streets of cities during Carnival.

Though the starting dates of Carnival vary from region to region, preparations for the holiday commonly begin on January 6, the Feast of the Epiphany. This is the day set aside to commemorate Jesus's presentation to the three wise men, or magi. Carnival

WORDS TO UNDERSTAND

Asceticism: Denying oneself things that give pleasure.

Masquerade: A formal party or dance, especially one that involves elegant masks and costumes.

Papier-mâché: Pieces of paper bonded with glue or flour and water used to make shapes and models.

Quinquagesima: The last Sunday before the beginning of Lent.

◀ Extravagent papier-mâché floats are some of the most exiciting sights during Carnival celebrations.

▲ **A float drives in the Rose Monday Carnival parade in Cologne, Germany.**

commonly ends with Ash Wednesday, the first day of Lent. The build-up to Ash Wednesday is a three-day period in which Carnival celebrations reach their climax. First to arrive on the Sunday before Lent is **Quinquagesima**, alternatively known as Dimanche Gras, Fat Sunday, or Shrove Sunday. In many countries this day is reserved as a respite from all festivities and an opportunity to meditate on the coming Lenten season. Following Quinquagesima is Fat Monday, also called Lundi Gras, Rose Monday, or Shrove Monday. In certain traditions it is a day for indulging in the meat, alcohol, and other things that will soon be forbidden during Lent.

However, in the Orthodox Church the day is known as "Clean Monday" and is reserved for confession of sins, cleaning of homes, and abandonment of foods barred by Lent. Fat Tuesday, often called Mardi Gras or Shrove Tuesday, comes next. This day is a high point of the Carnival season in cities worldwide. Parades, dances, and costume balls abound as people prepare themselves for the 40 days of rigorous **asceticism** ahead.

Experience the sights and sounds of a Mardi Gras celebration.

■ Music and Dancing

Live music is a crucial part of any Carnival celebration. It is selected to reflect the spontaneous and joyful atmosphere of the holiday. In some regions this means the playing of rhythmic, percussive instruments–such as conga drums–that lend themselves to freeform dancing. Other countries prefer to rekindle older, more traditional songs and dances that often hark back to indigenous or folk traditions. Musical performances spill out into the streets, absorbing the crowds and dissolving barriers between the performers and audience.

PREPARING FOR LENT

Prior to the beginning of Lent, people try to use up all the foods and products they are not allowed to eat once Lent begins, including many different animal products. Many people believe the days leading up to Ash Wednesday, the first day of Lent, earned the nickname *fat* because people try to use up animal fat on those days.

▲ A dance group performs in the streets during the Carnival in Barranquilla, Colombia.

■ Parades and Balls

Parades are another essential element of Carnival. They may include elaborate floats, people in costumes, and bands of musicians. Masquerades are an old holiday tradition in which people gather together in disguise, attempting to hide their true identities from one another for as long as possible. Though such traditions have declined over time, in recent years there have been resurgences of interest in old-fashioned masquerades during Carnival. Celebrants cite the sense of mystery and playfulness as motives for resurrecting this practice.

■ Food and Drink

Since ancient times, the joys of food and drink have been key parts of the traditions that have come to be known as Carnival. With the impending Lent, people use Carnival as a chance to indulge in all those foods that will soon be outlawed by their religious doctrines: meat, alcohol, eggs, milk, and sugar. There is a scramble to use up all these perishable foods before the onset

▲ Doughnuts are among the many different sweets and treats that celebrants indulge in leading up to Ash Wednesday and Lent.

of Lent. Thus in the days leading up to Ash Wednesday, celebrants concoct all sorts of recipes to use as many of these ingredients as possible. Doughnuts and pancakes are very popular in regions such as Britain, while pork feasts are prominent in Eastern European countries. Wine and spirits are consumed worldwide by those of age.

■ Conclusion

Carnival is a festive, joyful, and boisterous time with origins going as far back as antiquity. For many people, the excesses of Carnival are meant as preparation for the Lenten sacrifice ahead. However, over the years the meaning of Carnival has become as varied as its history. Though still a religious observance, the festival has evolved into an annual secular celebration of life in many places. In addition, while there are many similarities between celebratory traditions, each region

▲ A traditional Slovenian mask of Kurent. The mask is supposed to have supernatural power to chase away winter.

and culture that has adopted Carnival has put its own stamp on the holiday, often melding local and international customs. In this sense Carnival is an ever-evolving holiday that always sparkles with traces of its rich history and strong connections to the rituals of the past.

TEXT-DEPENDENT QUESTIONS

1: What does the Feast of the Epiphany commemorate?

2: Name two food products that are outlawed during Lent.

3: What are popular foods to eat before Lent in Britain?

RESEARCH PROJECTS

1: Research two or three foods consumed in the period leading up to Lent. Write a brief summary including the countries where they are consumed, the ingredients used, and any special variations of the recipe.

2: Research the Lundi Gras festival in New Orleans, Lousiana, including its history, its traditions, and some of its modern celebrations. Write a brief report summarizing your findings.

Celebrating in Europe

arnival is vigorously celebrated in European countries with sizable Catholoic populations, including Belgium, Denmark, England, France, Germany, Italy, Monaco, Portugal, Slovenia, Spain, and Switzerland. Each country incorporates traditions and practices from its own pre-Carnival and early Carnival celebrations. As a result, although the European celebrations include common elements such as parades, costumes, and musical performances, each country's Carnival is unique.

WORDS TO UNDERSTAND

Allegorical: Symbolic of some greater meaning, usually abstract.

Anonymity: When a person's name is not known or made public.

Choreograph: To design and direct something, especially pertaining to dance routines

Dialect: A form of language that changes slightly depending on the region.

Waltz: A type of ballroom dance involving simple steps that go around in a circle; a musical piece written for this dance.

◀ Carnival revelers in Florence, Italy, parade in native costumes of the Americas.

▲ A costumed Carnival reveler in Anguilas, Spain.

■ Carnival in Binche, Belgium

Carnival in the Belgian city of Binche, located about 34 miles south of Brussels (the Belgian capital), is celebrated three days before the beginning of Lent. While historians do not know the exact origin of today's Binche Carnival, most trace it back to Quaresmiaux, a pagan festival celebrating the change from winter to spring.

Many of the traditions of the Binche Carnival are unique, and the townspeople take great pride in them. Each year, a great number of tourists travel to Binche to join its residents in the Carnival celebration. Costumes play a major role in the festivities, and Binche's tradespeople supply fabrics, ribbons, feathers, and other necessary materials, giving a boost to the local economy.

GILLE COSTUMES INSPIRED BY THE PERUVIAN INCAS

One of the many traditional Carnival costumes is that of the Gille, or clown, which may be partly inspired by the traditional dress of the Peruvian Inca. As Binche legend has it, Mary of Hungary (the sister of Charles V, the king of Spain) had a castle built in Binche around the time of the Spanish conquest of Peru. In 1549, Mary hosted an elaborate party in her new castle in order to celebrate this recent conquest. The party featured many artifacts brought back from Peru, including samples of the great Inca culture the Spaniards had conquered. Some historians theorize that either several Incas traveled with the party procession, or that people attending Mary's party traveled to the castle costumed in traditional Inca dress, impressing the people of Binche so much that they copied the Inca attire in subsequent celebrations. Whatever the inspiration, the people of Binche began to incorporate a costume with similar elements, such as vertically embroidered patterns, into a yearly procession and celebration.

Today the Carnival performers are divided into different groups, called *societies*, each of which has its own musical band, Gille, and other costumed characters. Society members must meet many requirements, including being a native of Binche. These requirements ensure that the Binche Carnival retains its roots and remains authentic. There are even societies for children. These children are proud to serve as little Gilles and hope to one day be admitted into an adult Gille society.

CELEBRITY IMPERSONATION

Sometimes a society will choose a celebrity to poke fun at, especially if the celebrity has a distinctive way of dressing that makes him or her instantly recognizable. One year, for example, an entire society dressed as the famous German-born fashion designer Karl Lagerfeld. Each society member showed up costumed as a Lagerfeld look-alike, wearing large dark glasses and a powdered white wig tied back in a ponytail with a black ribbon. The Karl clones imitated the designer's signature look with a black-and-gray tie over a white shirt, numerous heavy silver rings showing under fingerless leather gloves, tight black pants, and a fake-diamond belt buckle spelling out "Karl." Some members carried silver-headed walking sticks or waved black lace fans.

PREPARING FOR THE BINCHE CARNIVAL

Public preparation for the Binche Carnival begins at least six weeks in advance with auditions and drum corps rehearsals for two successive Sundays. Other musicians attend practices called *soumonces* for four more Sundays. At each of these four rehearsals, another layer of complexity is added to the performance. After the drums play alone, dancers begin to work on their routines. Soon the brass band joins in. As the musical ensemble becomes more and more elaborate, so do

LEARNING CARNIVAL SONGS

Binche's Carnival musicians must often learn as many as 26 different Carnival songs!

the costumes of the musicians and dancers. Drummers begin by wearing normal street clothes then add a belt decorated with bells and wooden clogs, or *sabots*. By the final rehearsal, musicians are wearing their full costumes.

The final rehearsal occurs six days before the main festivities. On this special night, a ball called the Trouilles de Nouilles is held. The ball marks the first time during the Carnival season that people venture out in full costume.

The night is characterized by good-natured mischief. Most people try to disguise themselves completely so no one will guess their identity. Someone wearing a monkey's head might be arm in arm with a person who looks like a grandmother. Celebrants on this night take advantage of the **anonymity** granted by their masks and costumes to embarrass their neighbors and friends. This is known as *intriguing*. Behind their masks, they whisper rumors, disguising their voices. The person listening to the rumors is often unsure whether the speaker is passing on gossip he or she has heard from someone else, or simply making it up. The listener may feel unsettled, especially if the person in disguise mentions personal information.

DIMANCHE GRAS: CARNIVAL CELEBRATIONS BEGIN

After all the activities that precede the actual celebration are over and done with, Dimanche Gras finally arrives. Early in the morning, groups of drummers collect their society members and make their way to the main square. This is one of the most exciting moments of Carnival, as celebrants get to show off the spectacular costumes they have spent months preparing. Unlike the deliberately wacky or

CULTURAL TREASURE

The Binche Carnival is such a valuable cultural treasure that it has earned recognition on the United Nations UNESCO Heritage List.

outrageous costumes of Trouilles de Nouilles six days before, these costumes are works of art, sometimes costing several hundred dollars.

Each individual chooses his or her own costume, and common characters include the Pierrot and the Harlequin, from early European improvisational theater. The Pierrot, a dreamer who is unlucky in love and not very bright, dresses as a sad clown. The Harlequin (Arlequin in French), on the other hand, is known as being clever and witty, attractive to the ladies, although almost always short of money. He is easily recognizable in a close-fitting suit of multicolored diamond shapes. Traditionally, he wears a simple black mask over his eyes. Though poor, the Harlequin is usually much more successful at achieving what he wants than the Pierrot, thanks to his cleverness and charm.

There are other popular costumes as well; children dress as Peter Rabbit or Humpty Dumpty, and adults crowd the street costumed as peasants, pirates, magicians, genies, aristocrats, and monsters, as well as figures from popular culture such as Smurfs (blue animated cartoon characters still very popular in Europe today) or Star Wars Jedi knights. No Gilles are allowed to appear on this day, however. They must rest up for the activities that will take place on Mardi Gras.

LUNDI GRAS

Lundi Gras, or Fat Monday, is the time for private celebrations. Residents of Binche gather in groups of family and friends and visit cafés and people's homes. In the afternoon, young people march together, to the sound of the drums and brass bands, to the main plaza and on to the town hall. They engage in celebrations similar to those of the adults on Dimanche Gras. Later in the evening, they attend a fireworks display.

THE BIG CELEBRATION: MARDI GRAS

The most highly anticipated part of the festivities takes place on Mardi Gras, or Fat Tuesday. Members of the different Carnival societies don their traditional costumes (Harlequin, Pierrot, and peasant outfits) along with the Gilles who can on this day venture out for the first and only time. In addition to being the protagonists of the Carnival celebration, the Gilles represent the soul of the people of Binche. The rules of Carnival do not allow them to appear on any other day or in any other place. Only males are allowed to be Gilles.

The Gilles are unique to the Binche Carnival. Their costume includes a shirt and pants generally made from burlap, which is heavily embroidered with crowns, lions, and stripes in the traditional Belgian colors of black, red, and gold (the colors of the Belgian flag). Wire inside the shirt gives it a rigid structure and additional straw stuffed inside fills out the shirt, making the Gille look much more robust than the person inside the costume. Other elements of the costume include locally made, pointed wooden clogs and a cluster of bells that announce the arrival of the Gille even before he can be seen. A belt holds up bells that may weigh a total of five pounds or more. Another bell hangs from a ribbon around the Gille's neck. The traditional mask is probably the most peculiar part of the costume. The face of the wearer is hidden behind a wax mask, long orange sideburns, a curled-up moustache, and wire-rimmed spectacles.

▲ Children in traditional festive costume prepare to toss oranges to spectators during the Carnival parade in Binche, Belgium.

▲ Participants perform the Gilles of Binche dance during the Carnival in Binche, Belgium.

The festivities of Mardi Gras begin in the chilly predawn hours of the morning, when a few family members go to the home of the Gille to help him dress. For many

Watch a short documentary on the Binche Carnival.

Binchois, this is the best moment of Carnival because it involves the whole family working together, stuffing the Gille full of straw until he appears ready to burst. Eventually, the drummers of the Gille's society come to the door, playing the rhythmic pattern that will be heard throughout the day, and dancing the *pas de chat*, or "cat step." By now the Gille will have finished dressing. Turning carefully in his bulky costume, he dances slowly through his doorway to join the procession in the street. In this fashion, the group will go from house to house to collect each society member in what is known as the *ramassage*. The Gilles and their societies then make their way to the center of Binche to join all the other societies.

Since it is still dark in Binche when the societies gather, inhabitants and visitors in Binche hear the drums of the advancing societies long before they can make out the shadowy forms of the musicians and dancers. People fall in behind the marching societies. As more and more groups gather in the center of town, the noise and merriment grow until the rhythmic sound of the drums and wooden clogs, the excited laughter, and shouts of the crowd swell to a deafening level. By this

time the details of each costume are clearly visible in the morning light and the partying is well under way. At some point during the morning's festivities, the Gilles temporarily stop their dancing and refuel with a breakfast of champagne and oysters. The people of Binche save money during the year so that on Mardi Gras the Gilles can feast like kings.

One difference between a typical parade in North America and the one held in Binche is the interaction between the onlookers and those parading. In North America spectators are often separated from the performers by a cord or barrier, while in Binche, spectators dressed in costumes mingle with participants and children run

GILLE'S STATUE

In Binche, just beyond the Grand Place, there is a museum dedicated to the tradition of the Carnival. In front of the museum stands a sculpture of a Gille, complete with headgear. It was difficult for the sculptor to properly convey the feathery froth of the Gille's hat in metal, however. As a result, the statue, though immediately recognizable, does not compare with the appearance of the real thing.

▲ A Gille of Binche, Belgium, prepares to throw an orange to the public in celebration of Carnival.

happily around in the pandemonium, showering everyone they can reach with silly string or confetti. As a result, the parade moves very slowly, and everyone has to be patient as it makes its way through the city toward the Grand Place de Binche. Once in the Grand Place everyone watches the Gilles beat their drums, dance, and throw hundreds of oranges into the hordes of onlookers. Though nearby windows are covered with grilles to protect from this bombardment, some people in the nearby buildings deliberately stand in the windows, hold up screens like shields, and dare the Gilles to hit them. The Gilles usually oblige. Spectators catch as many oranges as they can, but inevitably some smash, and the scent of oranges fills the air.

During the afternoon celebration, the Gilles remove their masks and put on their towering ostrich-plume hats. This magnificent headwear stands almost four feet high and can weigh as much as seven pounds. Though boys can become Gilles if their parents permit them, most Gilles are adults. It takes strength and endurance to do all the walking and dancing that is required, especially with a frame stuffed with ostrich plumes on one's head and a heavy, bell-covered belt slung around one's waist. It is, however, the Gilles' headgear that is the most treasured sight of the Binche Carnival. From a distance, the bobbing white ostrich feathers of the crowd of Gilles look like a wave of foam sweeping slowly down the street. Awkward and heavy as their costumes may be, the Gilles will celebrate well into the night, which ends with a spectacular fireworks show and bonfire. This event is the grand finale of the Binche Carnival.

▲ Young revelers in costume for the Binche Carnival.

◼ Hot Times in France

Along the French Côte d'Azur (Blue Coast) parades are the focus during Carnival, with each town having its own slant on the holiday. It seems as if every location on the Côte d'Azur wants to celebrate the abundance that comes from the delightful Mediterranean climate.

PARADES AND FLOWER BATTLES IN NICE

A city in southeastern France, situated on the French Riviera, Nice (pronounced "niece") is home to an event called the Battle of the Flowers, in which people sitting on colorful floats throw flowers at the spectators. The audience members pick up the flowers and throw them back at the people on the floats, who duck, or hold up tennis or badminton rackets to protect themselves. Though the flowers are small and light, after a few hours of throwing and dodging flowers, everyone is pleasantly exhausted.

A version of the Nice Battle of the Flowers also takes place on the water in nearby Villefranche-sur-Mer, a seaport east of Nice. People enjoy looking at the boats decorated beautifully with local flowers such as carnations and mimosas, listening to live bands, and watching local performers. The parade in Nice also includes dummies with giant heads. The French call them *grosses têtes*. Often, the dummies will portray public figures, but with exaggerated features in playful mockery of the celebrity.

GOING BANANAS OVER LEMONS IN MENTON, FRANCE

Located on the French-Italian border, the town of Menton enjoys subtropical weather conditions and is the ideal place for growing citrus trees, palm trees, and mimosa flowers. At the end of the 19th century, the French Riviera was a popular vacation spot for the rich and famous–kings, princes, and artists were among those who came to escape the dreary winter of the North.

Menton was also the greatest source for citrus fruit on the continent. In 1929 a hotel owner had the clever idea of sponsoring a flower and citrus fruit exposition in the hotel to draw still more visitors to the area. His idea was so successful that two

Take a quick tour of the Menton Lemon Festival in France.

years later it became public in the form of a giant fruit parade. In 1934 this Lemon Festival, or Fête du Citron, which lasts three weeks, became an official Carnival event.

During three consecutive Sundays, floats pass along the Promenade du Soleil (Sun Promenade), decorated with oranges, limes, lemons, and any other kind of citrus fruit imaginable. Following a different theme each year, the fruit is carefully arranged into figures ranging from characters in *Alice in Wonderland* to a giant Buddha. One year a representation of even the Taj Mahal was made out of fruit. Every year the city invites a different country to visit and features that country's music and culture as part of the celebrations. For example, when Brazil was invited, the parade was accompanied by samba and bossa nova music. Dancers, majorette corps, and bands march between the groups of floats.

MENTON LEMON FUEL

Menton lemons are not ordinary lemons. They are fat and irregularly shaped, and their skin is not shiny like the lemons sold in American grocery stores. However in flavor they are the favorite of many talented chefs. And chefs are not the only ones convinced that Menton lemons are extraordinary. A former French race car driver who lives near Menton is supposedly working to develop a car fuel whose secret ingredient will be Menton lemon juice.

On other nights, the city sponsors moonlit parades followed by fireworks. Visitors who grow tired of the beach can also take in an orchid exhibition or crafts displays by local artists, or visit one of the largest citrus collections open to the public in Europe. These endangered species and rare plants are located in the garden of the former summer house of the Princes of Monaco, while the town's museum of fine arts is lodged in the house itself. (Menton was part of Monaco from the 14th century until 1848. It became part of France in 1860.)

In Menton's local Biovès gardens, giant citrus displays embody the theme, but in a form that visitors can admire any day during the weeks of Carnival. At night, special effects, music, and light shows cast a different spell. There are also festivities common to all the Carnival celebrations along the coast–concerts, parties, and firework displays. However, the organizers of the Menton lemon festival are very proud of how their Carnival differs from others. Unlike the many locations where parade floats are burned or thrown out after Carnival ends, Mentonese floats can be turned into jams, chutneys, and crystallized fruit.

■ The Many Faces of Carnival in Germany

The many differences between the Carnival holidays throughout Germany begin with their names. In the western German region of the Rhineland, where the cities of Cologne, Düsseldorf, and

▲ Visitors marvel at the beautiful scupltures at the Menton lemon festival.

Mainz are located, Carnival is called *Karneval*. In the southeast region of Bavaria, of which Munich is the capital, Carnival is called *Fasching*. In other areas of Germany it is known as *Fosnat*, *Fasnet*, and *Fastnacht*.

In general, 1823 is the date most often cited as the origin of the modern Karneval. In that year, an organization was founded to oversee the Karneval celebration. This body was the precursor to the modern Festive Committee, which today coordinates more than 100 Karneval associations and works to preserve the Karneval traditions. These holidays begin on different days in different parts of the country. In the Rhineland, perhaps the region with the best known Karneval celebrations, the Carnival season, known as "the fifth season," commences on the 11th minute of the 11th hour of the 11th day of the 11th month: 11:11 A.M., November 11th. The beginning of formalities matches the anniversary of the end of World War I, embodying the holiday's spirit of renewal and change that lies at the heart of peaceful relations among European powers today.

In the Rhineland customs similar to those of Karneval are known to have been observed as early as 1234. Historically, in Germany as in many other places, the rules of society were overthrown during this time. On Carnival Thursday during the week before Lent, towns recognize the Altweiber (old women) or Wieverfastelovend (the women's day). On this day, the women are in charge. Usually they begin by putting on fancy dresses, and at 10 A.M. they start heading for the town square. Often they storm city hall and take over the city council, other times they simply cheer

▲ Three women dressed as clowns dance at the old market in Cologne, Germany, on the first day of Carnival celebrations there.

and yell in the square. Men are careful to leave their favorite ties at home this day, because women will grab the ties and cut them from their shirts. In exchange, some women will deliver a kiss. In the evening, everyone attends parties and masked balls.

From Altweiber to Ash Wednesday, days continue in this festive spirit throughout the Rhineland. The highlight is the parade on Rose Monday, a variation of which takes place in nearly every city in the region. Hundreds of thousands of people come out, often dressed in costumes, to celebrate with song, dance, and by shouting the "Carnival cry" unique to their native city or town.

In Cologne, the three days before Ash Wednesday are known to be particularly rowdy. Throughout these three days, loud costume parades, masked balls, and a myriad of performances take place. Some people dress as jesters and go around playing pranks, while others perform plays, write newspaper columns, and give speeches that either poke fun at popular events or figures, or are completely nonsensical. As elsewhere in Rhineland, the main celebration is the Rose Monday parade three days before Lent. This parade, known in German as *Rosenmontag*, is led by the three Carnival figures of the Prince, the Peasant, and the Maiden.

Doughnuts called *fasnetskiechle* are a favorite treat throughout the Karneval season, in Cologne as well as the rest of Germany. The dough is made by mixing and kneading salt, flour, sugar, eggs, and a lot of cream. Then the cook rolls the dough flat, cuts it into squares, deep-fries the squares, and sprinkles them with powdered sugar.

■ Three Fun-Filled Days in Iceland

The three days of Bolludagur, Sprengidagur, and Öskudagur constitute the Icelandic version of Carnival. On Bolludagur ("Bun Day"), which takes place on the Monday before Ash Wednesday, children and adults alike indulge on delicious cream puffs. These "buns" are usually filled with custard or jelly and are sometimes covered in chocolate. Children begin Bolludagur by patting their sleeping parents with handmade bun wands to get them out of bed. For each successful (unblocked) tap of the wand, the parents give their child a cream puff.

FILLING UP ON MEAT AND PEAS

The name of Bursting Day (Sprengidagur) refers to the fact that people eat so much meat and peas that they feel as if they will burst.

Shrove Tuesday, known as Sprengidagur (Bursting Day), also involves a lot of eating. On this day, Icelandic people eat *saltkjot og baunir*, or salted meat and peas. The next day, Ash Wednesday, the children celebrate Öskudagur (Ash Day) by dressing in costumes and asking for candy. The day is much like Halloween in the United States, but with a slight twist: They must earn their candy by singing a song. Children also play a special prank on Ash Wednesday–they collect ash in a small bag and secretly try to attach it to someone's clothing.

■ Carnival in Venice, Italy

Carnival in the northern city of Venice is known in Italian as *Carnevale*. It may have begun as early as 1162, when Venice (at that time an independent republic) won a war against the forces of a man called Ulrico, the patriarch of Aquileia, an ancient Roman city on the Adriatic Sea. In celebration of the victory, the Venetians held a grand party in the plaza San Marcos, slaughtering 1 bull and 12 pigs for the feast. Historians believe this tradition continued for many years and eventually led to the development of Carnevale.

The first written record of mask wearing in Venice comes from a law in 1268 banning masqueraders from participating in the "egg" game. While historians do not know the details of the game, it was most likely messy and unruly. The anonymity provided by masks and costumes played an important role in Carnevale, because they allowed Venice's class structure to be upended.

The early times of the Venice Carnevale planted some traditions that are still followed today. Common activities included various forms of street entertainment–such as feats of strength, acrobatics, puppet shows, juggling demonstrations, musical performances, and fireworks displays, all of which were usually controlled by the state. Elegant private parties and costume balls often took place in wealthy aristocratic homes and palaces. Another popular pastime was gambling. Many state-run gambling houses were only open during Carnevale, and they brought in a great deal of revenue for the government.

By the latter half of the 15th century, Venice was one of the busiest seaports in the world. As Venice became a more powerful and popular city, its Carnevale also increased in size and grandeur. The city's artisans came to be famous for the beautiful masks and elegant costumes they created for Carnevale.

DECLINE AND FALL OF THE CARNEVALE

Leading into the 16th century, Venice began a steady decline in power. While the city's influence waned, its Carnevale became wilder. The outrageous and uninhibited celebration turned into a prime tourist destination for many young European aristocrats. Unfortunately, celebrations began to get out of control. Some revelers took advantage of the anonymity provided by masks and costumes to get away with immoral, illegal, and sometimes violent behavior. In response, legal records show that authorities were forced to rein in the uninhibited celebrations, especially regarding the costumes and masks. Soon laws forbade citizens to wear masks at night, in holy places such as churches, in casinos, and at any time of year other than Carnevale. Lawmakers also banned wearing a mask with religious attire, and carrying weapons while wearing a mask or costume.

FLIGHT OF THE TURK

One tradition that took place during the Carnevale of the past was the Flight of the Turk. In this event, which began in 1548 and ended in the last years of the 18th century, a Turkish tightrope-walker would walk up a tightrope tied from a boat in the bay of Saint Mark to the belfry of Saint Mark's Basilica, the most well-known church in Venice.

GAMBLING UNMASKED

Opening the gambling houses only during Carnevale season seemed like a good idea, because the wild, carefree Carnival atmosphere inspired the populace to be loose with its money. But problems did arise. Wearing costumes and masks had to be banned in the gambling houses, because too many people were betting anonymously and escaping unrecognized when they lost.

By the 18th century, the Venice Carnevale had reached its peak. The number of restrictions continued to mount, and the city's status continued to fall. In 1797, General Napoleon Bonaparte (later Napoleon I emperor of France), defeated the independent Venetian republic, and with it the glorious Carnevale. Venice fell under Austrian rule shortly after 1797, and then became part of the kingdom of Italy after 1866. Although Carnevale was held during this time, it continued to decline in significance, until the Italian dictator Benito Mussolini banned it completely in the 1930s.

◀ A traditional *bauta* mask worn during Carnival celebrations in Venice, Italy.

THE RESURRECTION OF CARNEVALE IN THE 1980s

It was not until the 1980s that the Venice Carnevale was revived. Since its reestablishment, it has gained recognition as a world-class festival. Today, Carnevale season offers the parades, musical performances, and theater shows for which it was once famous. The revival has also brought Venice's legendary tradition of elegant and intricate masks and costumes back to life.

Most people choose to dress up in traditional masks and costumes, such as the *bauta*, consisting of a long black robe, a tricornered hat, and a white mask that covers the entire face. This was a favorite during the heyday of the Venice Carnevale, because it guaranteed complete anonymity. Other popular costumes from Venice's past include the *moretta*, a black velvet mask sometimes worn by women; the *domino*, a long cape with a hood to cover the face; and various archetypal characters from Italian theater, such as a rich old merchant, a cunning servant, a foolish Harlequin, and a lazy goof-off known as Pulcinella.

Today, many of the celebrations are also organized for children, such as arts and crafts workshops, games, readings, treasure hunts, puppet shows, juggling performances, fancy costume parties, art competitions, traditional Venetian theater, comedy shows, parades, and even martial arts lessons accompanied by percussion instruments. Recent Carnevale celebrations have featured a great variety of musical performances: international groups combining traditional African and Celtic musical styles, marching bands, Scottish bagpipe corps, Latin American groups, jazz bands, and classical orchestras.

SWEET TREATS

Frittelle and *crostole*, two types of fried pastries, are enjoyed throughout the Carnevale season, and can be purchased in almost any pastry shop in Venice. *Frittele* are a type of fried dough balls made with yeast, flour, milk, eggs, sugar, and butter. Fruit is often added to the dough, including raisins, or pieces of lemon or apple. *Crostole* are a thinner pastry made with flour, eggs, sugar, butter, white wine, lemon, and a sweet liquor such as anisette, which tastes much like black licorice. After frying, both the *frittelle* and *crostole* are sprinkled with powdered sugar.

■ Six Hundred Years of Carnival in Monaco

Monaco, a small western European country flanked by France on two sides, has held Carnival since ancient times. In the early days of Carnival, children would dress up in old clothes. They would indulge in mock fights using rotten eggs, oranges, lemons, and chickpeas. Children would make dummies out of rags and straw and bounce them into the air using blankets. After the parade, the other Carnival celebrants would finish off the dummies by setting them aflame, and then dance through the night to the music of homemade instruments.

Carnival in Monaco may not have the humble elements it did a long time ago, but the traditions of today still embody the fun, carefree attitude of the holiday. Monacans clad in colorful attire and wearing masks parade through the streets of the principality. Musical bands play music nonstop, and singing, dancing, and feasting take place. There are also attractions such as flower-covered floats and parades of giant balloons along the beach, often with a marine theme. Given that this region along the Mediterranean enjoys approximately 300 days of sunshine a year, the weather only enhances the spirited day.

■ Carnival in Portugal

The Portuguese celebrate Carnival with much gusto. Like other countries, the Carnival celebration in Portugal reaches its apex in the three days prior to Ash Wednesday with parades, music, dancing, and singing. *Caretos*, or masked figures, weave in and out of the parades, stopping to interact with people as they move through the streets of cities and towns. Portugal has borrowed some Carnival traditions–such as samba dancing and heavily percussive music–from Brazil, which was once its colony. At the end of Carnival, some towns in Portugal take part in the pagan ritual of *entrudo*.

Entrudo, associated with freedom, role-reversals, and letting off steam, is believed to have originated in Dionysian revels in Rome and come to Portugal in the 15th century. Originally, revelers threw perfume-filled balls of wax, eggs, and starch at each other–though it is likely that only the wealthy could afford the perfume.

A GIANT SAMBA PARADE ON MADEIRA, PORTUGAL

Many cities in Portugal stage Carnival celebrations, but one of the largest takes place in Funchal, the capital of Madeira, a

CREATING ANTICIPATION FOR CARNIVAL

One month before the peak of Carnival in Monaco, the dancers and performers visit hotels and entertain the guests with their routines. The dancers are hoping to create anticipation for Carnival and to build a following of fans.

Portuguese island in the Atlantic. The most important parade of the festivities occurs on the Saturday before Ash Wednesday. Known as the **allegorical** parade, it requires a lot of commitment and organization from everyone involved. Costumes must be prepared for the thousands of participants who will be dressed in all colors of the rainbow and adorned with feathers, beads, glitter, sequins, masks, and matching footwear. In addition, dances are **choreographed** and taught to about 1,500 dancers. The electrifying music and dancing is mostly samba. Most of the performers in the allegorical parade are members of samba groups who are competing to see who can give the best performance on the streets of Funchal. One of their goals is to be so lively and engaging that they can persuade the tourists and bystanders to dance.

The merriment continues on Shrove Tuesday when Carnival-goers don costumes of famous people and go out on the town. During the second parade, named Cortejo Trapalhão (Trickster Parade), revelers have a chance to poke fun at people such as traditional characters in Madeiran life, or politicians of past and present. Everyone can take part, and there is much more improvisation than during the allegorical parade. This is also a time when people who live in Madeira may see a new side to people they know. Everyone seems more daring during the Trickster Parade in imaginative costumes. Many bars and clubs also host musical performances this night.

■ Carnival in Mainland Portugal

CELEBRATION IN TORRES VEDRA

Mainland Portugal celebrates Carnival in ways similar to Madeira, but with some notable differences. For one thing, the mainland is colder than Madeira in February, so costumes are less revealing. The Portuguese city Torres Vedra, which is located on Portugal's west coast, is reputed to put on the best Portuguese Carnival. Here the parades resemble Madeira's Cortejo Trapalhão much more than they do its allegorical parade.

In Torres Vedra, a current issue often becomes the theme for Carnival–for example, turmoil in the Middle East or global warming. This helps the float makers come up with groupings of well-known figures they can arrange on the floats–usually politicians such as the president of the United States and Britain's prime minister, but sometimes local figures too. Frequently the authority figures

CLEAN COSTUMES

One year, the prize for best costume in Cabanas de Viriato, Portugal went to a group of people dressed as mops.

▲ Carnival particpants wear wooden masks in Lazarim, Portugal.

are represented by exaggerated papier-mâché sculptures. Typically, everyone participates in the mainland Portugal Carnival parades. Fewer music and dance competitions are held here than on Madeira, and there are fewer organized samba groups. This allows people to celebrate without first learning specific routines. Indeed, the spontaneous celebrating in Torres Vedra can make other Carnivals look over-choreographed.

FOLK DANCING IN CABANAS DE VIRIATO

One of the more informal Carnivals takes place in the town of Cabanas de Viriato in northern Portugal. Most of the costumes are homemade and show amazing inventiveness and creativity. The town's celebrations include two popular contra dances–folk dances in which two long lines of people face each other. Though the dancers may go through a variety of patterns and switch partners during the dance, they usually end up opposite their original partners.

One of the contra dances, humorously called the Danças dos Cús, or "Butt Dance," is performed on each of three days during Carnival. As the band plays a lively **waltz**, each pair of dancers whirls into the space separating them, bumps hips, and then dances back into the line. In between, several bump steps are traveling steps that allow the dancers to move forward. The dance has become so popular and the lines of dancers so long that the music is now broadcast over loudspeakers so everyone can hear.

■ Pust Is Carnival in Slovenia

In Slovenia, which is 58 percent Roman Catholic, the Carnival celebration is called *Pust*. Pust is characterized by a riotous atmosphere that grips the entire nation, as people dress in colorful costumes to celebrate the day before the beginning of Lent. *Krof* (a marmalade doughnut) is an integral part of Pust celebrations and is popular among children.

◀ Performers wearing the Slovenian masks of Kurent dance in the yard of a house in a Slovenian village. The mask is supposed to have supernatural power to chase away winter and usher in spring.

One of the most famous Pust celebrations is held in the city of Cerknica. Here, people dress as witches and monsters and participate in daylong parades. Children feast on candies, sweets, and sausages and enjoy the fun-filled atmosphere. An important figure in Pust is Kurent, a creature with a long red nose who wears a hedgehog skin and carries a staff. Kurent is believed to drive away the winter and usher in spring, abundant crops, and plentiful harvests.

■ Carnival in the Port Cities of Spain

Since the majority of Spain is Roman Catholic, many towns hold Carnival celebrations that include costume balls, folk dances, and fireworks in the evenings.

The most famous of the Carnival celebrations are held in the port cities of Cádiz and Santa Cruz de Tenerife. The Carnival celebrations in both Cádiz and Santa Cruz were shaped by their locations. Today they attract a huge number of visitors to the country every year.

CÁDIZ HAS VENETIAN AND SPANISH FLAVORS

Because of its location near the entrance to the Mediterranean Sea, the city of Cádiz was a frequent trading partner of Venice, Italy, during the 16th century. At this time Venice was an independent republic. Since Cádiz and Venice were trading partners during the 16th century, the Spanish city adopted certain Venetian Carnivale traditions such as the wearing of masks and singing of comedic songs. Cádiz also served as a stopping point for Spanish ships returning from colonies in the Americas and the Caribbean. In addition to gold and silver, Spanish explorers returned with samplings of the culture and music of the Caribbean, which by the mid-17th century already had considerable African and Creole influence. Some of these cultural elements, such as samba music, made their way into the Cádiz Carnival. Today, the Cádiz Carnival features parades, costumes, music, and dancing. Singing groups compete against one another for the best costume and original song, usually written about a current topic in the news.

SANTA CRUZ DE TENERIFE FOCUSES ON KIDS

Located on Tenerife, the largest of the Canary Islands, just off the west coast of northern Africa, the city of Santa Cruz was another frequent stopping point for ships traveling between Europe and the Americas. Naturally, its Carnival celebration took on elements from both places. The Santa Cruz Carnival is geared toward children, who compete on beautifully decorated stages in elaborate costumes for music, dance, and other performing arts prizes.

▲ The carnival queen of Santa Cruz de Tenerife's Carnival stands on the platform of the float in the capital of the Spanish Canary Island of Tenerife parade.

■ Basler Fasnacht in Switzerland

Long before the modern Carnival began, people in Switzerland celebrated a spring festival meant to drive away evil spirits. People paraded around in ugly masks and played loud music that is perhaps better described as an awful racket. Later, this celebration became a day dedicated to the patron saint of the village. This predecessor to today's Carnival has contributed to the pre-Lenten celebrations throughout Switzerland.

Today, the largest Carnival celebration in Switzerland takes place in Basel and draws

CARNIVAL TREATS IN BASEL

Carnival in Basel, a city in Switzerland, does not include the sweets typical of other Carnival celebrations. Instead, the three main dishes are a broth made from flour and onions, cheese, and onion pies.

▲ Carnival fools walk with masks, lanterns, drums, and flutes during the Morgestraich Carnival procession through the streets of Basel, Switzerland.

more than 10,000 spectators and celebrants. Known as Basler Fasnacht, the festival is traditionally held on the first Monday after Ash Wednesday. Basler Fasnacht is one of the few celebrations held after the beginning of Lent. Although no one seems to know how this came to be, some point to the city's adoption of Protestantism as a possible contributing factor; as Ash Wednesday and Lent lost significance celebrants differentiated from older Catholic traditions.

The celebrating begins in the freezing cold at four in the morning when groups of drummers and flutists parade through the streets. At this hour, while it is still dark, the streetlamps are turned off and the procession is illuminated with massive decorative lanterns. Celebrants wear vibrant masks and costumes and dance and party all day long. One popular costume is that of an ugly devil with long, curved horns and a bright red tongue that hangs out of his mouth. As in Carnivals elsewhere, revelers poke fun at local personalities and events with costumes, songs, and rhyming poems, written in the local **dialect**.

TEXT-DEPENDENT QUESTIONS

1: Where is the city of Binche?

2: Describe the differences between the Harlequin and Pierrot Carnival costumes.

3: What is the special Carnival tradition in Menton, France?

4: What foods are consumed on Shrove Tuesday in Iceland?

5: How do people celebrate Carnival in Cabanas de Viriato in Portugal?

RESEARCH PROJECTS

1: Research some of the customs of Switzerland's Basler Fasnacht Carnival celebration, including popular costumes, musical groups and concerts, floats, and other traditions. Write a brief synopsis of a typical Basler Fasnacht celebration.

2: Select a European nation or geographical region not covered in this chapter, such as Lithuania, Sicily (a part of Italy), or the Czech Republic. Research Carnival traditions particular to that area, including food, dance, music, floats, and other customs. Write a brief report summarizing your findings.

Celebrating in Latin America and the Caribbean

As the last blowout before the Christian holiday of Lent, Carnival is the biggest and most eagerly awaited event of the year in many countries throughout Latin America and the Caribbean. The festivities, which include parades, and a lot of eating and drinking and last anywhere from a few days to an entire month, are colorful, loud, and great fun. Revelers dress in costumes, wear masks, and dance in the streets to pounding rhythmic music. They compete for best costume, best music, best poetry, and, most important, the titles of king and queen of Carnival. Local celebrations are as diverse as the region itself.

WORDS TO UNDERSTAND

Abolish: To bring an end to something.

Appliqué: Cloth decorations that are sewn or attached on to other articles of clothing.

Improvise: To perform or speak without prior preparation.

◀ The display of devil costumes is common in places like Bolivia.

THE ARRIVAL OF KING VAVAL

In French Guiana, Guadeloupe, and Martinique—where Carnival celebrations date back to the abolition of slavery in 1848—festivities start with the arrival of King Vaval, a large puppet representing the spirit of Carnival. King Vaval arrives in a canoe and is met by a large crowd gathered on the beach to welcome him. The two weeks of festivities officially end on Mardi Gras with the burning of King Vaval.

In places such as Bolivia, Guadeloupe, Martinique, and Venezuela dressing and dancing in devil costumes is common. The dancing devils represent the sins that Carnival is supposed to wash away before the beginning of Lent and the Easter season. A symbolic straw figure reigns over Carnival in many Caribbean countries. This straw mannequin, which symbolizes flesh, is often carried at the head of the main parade and is then burned in a big bonfire at the close of Carnival. The ritual ceremony is meant to burn away the sins of the people before Lent. Often, the ashes from the burned straw doll are used to mark the sign of the cross on the foreheads of the Christian faithful on Ash Wednesday, the day Carnival ends.

■ A Unique Mix of Cultures

Many countries in Latin America and the Caribbean have populations made up mostly of the descendants of three groups: the indigenous peoples who lived there before Europeans arrived, European colonizers, and Africans, whom the Europeans brought to the region as enslaved laborers. Because these groups contributed their traditions to the developing societies of Latin America and the Caribbean, those societies became a blend of many cultures. Former French colonies such as Haiti, Guadeloupe, and Martinique speak French and have a French form of government, but they also embrace deep African roots in music, food, and religion. Similarly, former Spanish colonies such as Venezuela, Argentina, and Mexico combine Spanish customs with those of African origin as well as those of the indigenous peoples, who have lived there and mixed with European populations since before the arrival of the Europeans.

The blend of traditions is perhaps most striking in religion. Carnival was introduced to Latin America and the Caribbean as a Christian holiday by European colonists. The indigenous peoples and the enslaved Africans came from non-Christian traditions. Although much of the population of Latin America and the Caribbean is Christian today, the people of each region have developed their own distinct religious traditions. In many places in Latin America and the Caribbean, Carnival celebrations fuse Christian practices with multiple native traditions that are older than Christianity.

■ Carnival and the Liberation of Enslaved People

The masquerades and dances that are so important to Carnival developed from the days of slavery. Such activities were a feature of the French plantation culture on islands in the Caribbean. Families would visit one another for parties between Samedi Gras and Mardi Gras (Fat Saturday and Fat Tuesday). When slavery was **abolished** in the French colonies in 1848, the freed slaves took these plantation parties to the streets, creating a celebration similar to today's Carnival.

REGGAE, SOCA, MENTO, AND THE STEEL BANDS

Reggae is of Jamaican origin and emerged in the late 1960s, building on the traditions of ska (Jamaican music that became popular in the 1950s). Reggae emphasizes the back-beat; the rhythm guitarist is vital to this music. Bob Marley (1945–81) played a spiritual style known as *roots reggae*.

Soca is a blend of slower soul music beats and quick rhythms. Introduced in the 1970s, it became an essential part of Carnival within a decade. Mento is a type of Jamaican folk music that provided the foundation for music that followed it, such as ska and reggae. Mento has African origins and is played mostly on acoustic instruments, such as guitar, banjo, hand drums, and rhumba box–an instrument based on the African *mbira* (a thumb piano), but large enough to sit on. Mento and calypso are similar, but mento does not have the Spanish influence that came from Trinidad and Tobago. Mento was at its most popular during the 1950s.

Steel bands play on hammered metal pans made from empty 55-gallon oil drums. Once the drum is cut apart, the panmaker uses a 40-pound sledgehammer to beat the bottom into the dish shape known as *the pan*. The next step is to temper the pans by heating and then cooling them. The final steps involve tuning and painting the drums. The musicians make different notes by hitting the pans in different places.

Slaves born in the West Indies had no firsthand connection to their African roots. Stories, music, and dances learned from their elders were their only link to the culture from which they had come. In the latter 1800s freed slaves were still not allowed to participate in the celebrations of the Europeans, so they held their own celebrations, which often mocked their former masters. The events also celebrated their cultural heritage. The freed slaves dressed up in costumes and masks that represented characters from African myths. They would also sing and dance to African music.

■ Summer Carnival in Antigua and Barbuda

While most countries celebrate Carnival in February to mark the beginning of the Christian Lent season, the Caribbean island nation of Antigua and Barbuda holds a Carnival during summer. This is because the holiday commemorates Britain's Emancipation Act of 1834, which freed approximately 670,000 slaves in the West Indies. The act required the newly freed slaves to serve four-year apprenticeships to their former owners–essentially an extension of slavery. Antigua and Barbuda was the only country where the slaves were freed without being forced into these apprenticeships.

The island country celebrates the emancipation of its people with a lively 10-day event that takes place in late July and culminates in a parade on the first Tuesday in August. Concerts, food fairs, parades, and other cultural shows are organized throughout, but the most spirited festival takes place in the capital city of Saint John's. This celebration features many different types of music, such as calypso, soca, reggae, and steel bands. Some events are the Parade of Costumed Bands, Caribbean Queen, Miss Antigua Pageant, Party Monarch, and Calypso Monarch. Masquerades are held as well.

■ Devil Doll in Argentina

In northern Argentina, Carnival is still observed by people of the Andes Mountains in part as a celebration of the harvest. The festival begins when the *algarroba* (carob) beans have ripened. A small devil doll (brought out each year) is dug out of its rocky home in the mountains and decorated with cornhusks and flowers to represent the harvest. Once the doll appears, boys dressed like the devil toss it about and then, followed by a band, carry it in a procession through the streets to the town hall. Singing–accompanied by *charangos*, related to the guitar and ukeleles–can be heard throughout the village. On the Thursday before Lent, women form two lines–one for mothers, the other for grandmothers–and meet under an arch of fruit, cheese, tiny lanterns, and sweets. There, the women exchange a doll that is touched to each woman's forehead. This ceremony unites the women in a lifelong bond.

▲ People dressed as devils dance during Carnival in a small town in Argentina. Carnival is seen as the chance for villagers to offer their thanks to Pachamama, or Earth Mother, for all she has given to them.

Carnival reaches its high point on Sunday, when women wear traditional clothes: wide ruffled skirts, colorful ponchos, and white hats. They mask their faces with talcum powder and water. Riding on horseback and singing folksongs, they arrive at the dance held in honor of Pukllay, a supernatural being representing the spirit of Carnival. The word *Pukllay* means "game" in Quechua, the language spoken by indigenous people of the Andes Mountains. When the celebrations end, the devil doll that represents Pukllay is reburied, symbolizing the end of Carnival.

■ Burning King Momo in Aruba

In Aruba, preparations and events begin months in advance with a calypso competition at the end of January; a steel band competition follows to determine which bands will participate in the parade held in Oranjestad, Aruba's capital city. The Carnival festivities culminate with the main event the Grand Carnival parade, which is always the Sunday before Mardi Gras. It begins at 11 A.M. in Oranjestad and takes about eight hours to make its way through the streets of the city. The Old

▲ A costumed performer celebrates Carnival in Oranjestad, Aruba.

Mask Parade is lead by King Momo, the symbolic straw figure who reigns over Carnival. When King Momo is burned at the parade's end, he takes the sins of the people with him, leaving the island pure. The burning of King Momo must take place before midnight on Tuesday, signifying the end of Carnival and the start of Lent. Momo's ashes are used on Ash Wednesday to mark the sign of the cross on the foreheads of churchgoing Christians.

■ La Diablada in Bolivia

In Bolivia Carnival is an occasion of great festivity, with celebrants spilling over into the streets of all major towns in the country. In the Bolivian town of Santa Cruz people dress as devils in wild costumes and plaster masks and dance *la diablada* (the devil's dance). After the dance, Catholics go to church, where a priest blesses them. The next day they attend mass and once again perform

▲ Bolivian devil dancers perform a traditional *diablada* dance during Carnival celebrations.

▲ Dancers wear traditional costumes and dance at Diablada Oruro Carnival in Bolivia.

la diablada. In 1789, it is said that the Virgin Mary appeared at the top of a silver mineshaft in the city of Oruro; since then, Bolivian Carnival has had a special significance in that it honors this "Virgin of the Mineshaft" as well as all those miners who have lost their lives in mining accidents. Since mining is a significant part of the Bolivian economy, this is a means of connecting the Carnival tradition with other, more national and historical narratives.

■ Carnaval in Brazil

Brazil's Carnival (or Carnaval, as it is written in Portuguese) is world-famous for its unrestrained atmosphere of jubilant celebration. The four-day party represents the wildest celebration that Brazil, and possibly all of South America, has to offer. Brazil's history has given birth to a distinctive Carnaval celebration. Here, the traditional Roman Catholic holiday of Carnival was enhanced by the rituals and customs of the descendants of African people who were brought to the Portuguese colony. This new blend of holidays and traditions developed mainly in the cities of coastal Brazil from Recife to Rio de Janeiro.

▲ A costumed man takes part in the gala in the streets of Rio de Janeiro, Brazil. The Rio Carnival, a four-day wild party of dancing, singing, and parades practically shuts down the entire city each year.

FROM MUDFIGHTS TO SAMBA MUSIC

The Brazilian Carnaval probably began sometime in the 18th century as an imported form of the Portuguese *entrudo* celebration. In this festival, people would take to the streets and engage in a glorified water fight. While it may sound harmless, it often became messy and dangerous. Combatants would add limes, limejuice, flour, and dirt, engaging in a wet food fight with a little mud thrown in. These celebrations did not always end happily or peacefully. Today's Carnaval, however, focuses more on fun and less on filth.

As in other countries, Portuguese revelers began to hold masked balls during Carnaval. The first of these was held in 1840 by the upper classes at the Hotel Italia and featured European music such as the waltz and polka. A young Portuguese shoemaker named José Nogueira de Azevedo Paredes is commonly credited with beginning a new Carnaval ritual just a few years after the first ball. His idea was to march through the streets playing the drum, welcoming others to join him with their own musical instruments. Those who played this spontaneous street music came to be known as Zé Pereiras, which is probably a distortion of the name José Paredes. His idea took off, and the first official, organized parades appeared in 1850 and featured military bands and horse-drawn floats.

From this time through the end of the 19th century, the celebration of Carnaval became more democratic and included people of all social classes. This was a change from the earlier days of the celebration, when Carnaval was only open to those of the upper class. Partly as a result of the abolition of slavery in Brazil in 1888 (Brazil was the last country in the world to outlaw slavery), many people of African descent moved to Rio and other cities in search of employment. They began to develop their own way of observing the holiday, namely by parading through the streets playing African-influenced music and dancing. The groups of men who participated in the parades were called *cordões*, and they often celebrated violently. Later groups called *ranchos* included women and acted in a more refined manner. Their parades were the first to incorporate themes—such as stories of famous figures, reenactments of important events, or political messages—a practice common in today's Carnaval.

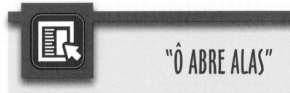

"Ô ABRE ALAS"

"Ô Abre Alas" was the first song written specifically for Carnaval in Brazil. Because of its infectious rhythm and simple lyrics–which made it easy to sing along to–it was a huge hit. Here is the chorus:

Hey, make way
I want to pass
I like parties
I can't deny that

The Carnaval of 1899 featured the first song written exclusively for the holiday. This upbeat song, entitled "Ô Abre Alas" (Make Way), was the first of many musical developments to emerge from Carnaval, including the *marcha* and the samba that originated around 1917. A mix of many other musical styles, the *marcha* and the samba probably developed in the slums of Rio, known as the *favelas*. The poor people of these neighborhoods most likely drew from African, European, and Latin American musical traditions when composing the music now known as *samba*. In addition to inventing these new musical styles, the poor people of Rio became the driving force behind Carnaval.

THE REVOLUTION OF THE SAMBA SCHOOLS

Lively and rhythmic, samba music and dance became the backbone of the Brazilian Carnaval. The first *escola de* samba (samba school) was organized in 1928 by a group of men of African descent who wanted to make music and perform in a parade during Carnaval. Although this first samba school only lasted a few years, it started a tradition that endures today.

▲ One of the samba schools marches at the Sambadrome in Rio de Janeiro, Brazil.

The *escolas* continued to increase in number, and in 1935 the Brazilian government dropped its opposition to the schools and began to recognize them. For many years the samba parades were held in the center of Rio, with temporary grandstands lining the streets. But eventually the celebration outgrew the congested city center, and in 1984 the parades were moved to the newly constructed Sambadrome, a stadium with a capacity of 85,000 spectators. Today the *escolas*, which number more than 50 in Rio alone, do much more for

OSCAR NIEMEYER

The Sambadrome (or Sambódromo in Portuguese) was designed by Oscar Niemeyer, an internationally acclaimed Brazilian architect. Niemeyer was also involved in the planning and construction of the new Brazilian capital city, Brasilia, from 1956 to 1961. He designed many government buildings in Brasilia.

the community than just teach dance. A large number of *escolas* serve as social and recreational centers, providing health care services and supporting local schools and child care centers. A few corrupt schools are involved in illegal activities such as gambling, but generally the schools have generated tremendous community pride and unity. The *escolas* support themselves through contributions, membership fees, and proceeds from their performances and other fund-raisers.

Today the enormous samba competition held in the Sambadrome generates a great deal of business for various industries, including costume makers, float designers, and craftsmen such as carpenters and painters. The largest *escolas* have several thousand members, most of whom participate in the parade and dance competition, each wearing an elaborate costume. The *escolas* compete for a cash prize and, more important, the right to be called the finest samba school in the nation. Organizing this event is quite a challenge and requires the help of directors for different aspects of the performance—such as the drumming, the singing, and the choreography. The best songs are recorded on CDs and sold nationwide. Winning can bring great fame and profit to a school.

BIGGEST CARNIVAL IN THE WORLD IN RIO DE JANEIRO

The Rio de Janeiro Carnaval is by far the largest in Brazil, and probably the largest in the world. The main parade, which is also a samba competition, became so big that the Sambadrome was constructed to host it. Rio's Carnaval has become an increasingly popular tourist attraction, and yearly visitors are estimated in the hundreds of thousands. In addition to enjoying the event itself, tourists from the Northern Hemisphere looking to escape winter cold can bask in the Brazilian summer.

Many Rio residents who are not practicing members of a samba school can neither afford nor obtain tickets to the Sambadrome, so they focus on celebrating Carnaval on the streets and beaches of Rio. Parades and dance contests are held all around the elaborately decorated city, and long processions of dancers crowd the streets as well as the two popular beaches of Copacabana and Ipanema.

CARNIVAL CELEBRATIONS ON A SMALLER SCALE IN SALVADOR DA BAHIA AND RECIFE

Many other Brazilian cities also host grand Carnaval celebrations. Due to the commercialization of the Rio Carnaval, many people prefer to visit smaller Carnavals that may be more authentic. Two of the better but not-too-well-known Carnaval cities are Salvador da Bahia and Recife. All of the ceremonies in Salvador take place publicly, on the streets, and all performers sing and play for fun rather than for money. Small groups called *electrical trios* play out of the beds of pickup trucks that drive through the city. Other, larger groups, sometimes with as many as 40 musicians, play out of tractor-trailer trucks. Salvador was the center of the slave trade during Brazil's slavery era, which lasted from the mid-16th to the end of the 19th century. As a result, the city's culture reflects African traditions much more than other Brazilian cities. This heritage is particularly visible in the city's Carnaval festivities, which move to the rhythms of African music played on traditional African instruments. Participants are proud to wear costumes inspired by their cultures of origin.

■ Carnival in the Dominican Republic

Carnival in the Dominican Republic is the most colorful festival of the year. Not only is it a time of feasting before Lent, but it often coincides with Independence Day. The importance of family is stressed as men, women, and children of all ages dressed up as various characters participate in parades. Families may also get together to make small floats and adorn them with an array of found objects such as colored cardboard or fruit. The parades wind their way through towns, villages, and cities of all sizes, always ending in the locality's central square. By far the most popular character in these parades is the devil, known as Diablo Cojuelo. He lashes out at onlookers with an inflated cow bladder known as a *vejiga* to purge them of their sins. It is believed that he is based on a character in the Spanish novel *Don Quixote* by Miguel de Cervantes. Since the Dominican Republic was once a colony of Spain, it is very probable that this work came to influence its Carnival celebrations, with other cultures influenced by the Spanish, such as Puerto Rico's, also making use of the cow bladder in celebrating Carnival.

Water Balloon Fights in Ecuador

Throughout Ecuador, water balloon fights are popular during Carnival, mostly with children and teenagers. Often the balloons are filled not with water but with much messier materials, such as flour or eggs. The government has tried to ban water balloon fights, but because of their popularity, the government has trouble effectively enforcing its decision to abolish them.

Carnival Queens in French Guiana

In French Guiana, Carnival is called *Tululu*. Carnival celebrations, which began in 1848 after the abolition of slavery, span two weeks. They end on Mardi Gras, the day before Ash Wednesday. During Carnival in the capital city of Cayenne and other parts of French Guiana, people dress up in colorful outlandish costumes, participate in parades, and attend the many parties that are being held. Carnival starts with the arrival of King Vaval, an effigy representing the spirit of Carnival. Vaval arrives in a canoe and is met by a large crowd gathered on the beach to welcome him. At the end of Ash Wednesday King Vaval is set ablaze.

The most important Carnival characters here are the Carnival queens, known as *Touloulous*. These women wear masks and dress from head to toe in lace and petticoats, tights, and gloves. They even disguise their voices when they speak so as not to be recognized. On Friday and Saturday nights of Carnival, the Touloulous gather at large dance halls called *universities*. Men are invited but must pay a fee to enter. The scene is similar to the costume balls that take place in other countries during Carnival, as the Touloulous talk, dance, and gossip with the men in total anonymity.

Competing for Best Calypso Poet in Grenada

Carnival in Grenada begins in July with the National Calypso Monarch Competition in which calypso poets, young and old alike, recite their poems amid colorful celebrations. Calypso was originally a means of communication for enslaved field workers. Because they were not allowed to speak to one another while working, they developed a musical code, which evolved over the years to often include satire of local figures.

In the competition, the calypsonian (soloist) is the main artist who has to combine the distinctive musical styles of different tribes into one lyrical piece to be performed. An expert calypsonian is like a skilled jazz musician. Through extensive knowledge of the musical form of calypso, he or she is able to **improvise** quickly, coming up with new lyrics on the spot.

■ Dancing Wolves in Guadeloupe

The Sunday before Carnival in Guadeloupe there are dancing, masquerades, and a good deal of excitement in the streets. On Shrove Tuesday, masqueraders parade, dressed in pajamas, and dance all day long. The theme for the parades changes every year. On Ash Wednesday, the streets are filled with revelers dressed in black-and-white wolf costumes. Carnival comes to a close on Ash Wednesday when King Carnival, in his Vaval manifestation, is burned to the sound of loud wails from the assembled crowd. Dinner and dancing follow.

In Guadeloupe, Carnival is also revived for one day, midway between Carnival and Easter. On this day revelers dress up as devils in red-and-black costumes.

■ Vodun Musical Celebrations in Haiti

Of all Caribbean Carnival celebrations, Haiti's is the most definitively African. It incorporates many elements of Vodun, a religion that has roots in traditional African beliefs. *Rara* (Vodun music) is prominent at the Carnival parades and features percussion instruments such as bells, drums, maracas, and shakers. Most of the instruments are homemade. The dancers and musicians wear

▲ Natives dressed in traditional costume dance in the streets during Carnival festivities in Martinique.

▲ As opposed to most Carnivals, which end with the beginning of Lent, Haiti's Rara Carnival is celebrated in the countryside by members of Vodun societies during the 40 days of Lent.

bright costumes to represent the strength of their protective Iwa (Vodun clan spirit). They believe that their Iwa protects them from the Iwa of other groups.

After the end of Carnival and throughout the 40-day fasting period of Lent, *rara* celebrations are held every weekend throughout the countryside. Musical bands with brightly costumed dancers and musicians move slowly through the streets, picking up people along the way. *Rara* celebrations may appear disorganized, but strict rules govern the dancing.

■ Carnival in Martinique

In Martinique, Carnival is both a religious and a public holiday. The official beginning of Carnival is Samedi Gras (Fat Saturday), when people attend parties and dance all night long. King Vaval, a giant mannequin, is the king of Carnival and is featured, along with beautiful floats and revelers, in the big parade on Dimanche Gras (Fat Sunday). Lundi Gras (Fat Monday) is the day of the "Mock Wedding." On this day, men dress as women and women as men. These costumes are worn to the series of masked balls that last late into the evening. Mardi Gras (Fat Tuesday) is known as Red Devils Day. On this day people wear red-devil costumes adorned with shimmering silver and sparkling decorations, as well as bells that jingle as they dance in the streets till sunset. Martinique is one of three countries in the world where Carnival does not end on, or before, Ash Wednesday.

Instead, it ends in the early morning hours after Ash Wednesday. At the end of the day, as in French Guiana and Guadeloupe, a straw puppet of King Vaval is burned.

■ Confetti-Filled Eggs in Mexico

Carnival is celebrated for five days in Mexico. While enjoying parades, dances, religious processions, fireworks, food, and traditional Mexican music, revelers have to be on the lookout for *cascarones* (confetti-filled eggshells) tossed at them by other partygoers. The eggs are hollowed out and dried, then painted fun colors and filled with brightly colored confetti. People believe that having confetti eggs cracked on their heads brings them good luck. Many people also believe that the egg symbolizes Jesus emerging from the tomb because baby chicks emerge from the dark interior of an egg into the light.

▲ Confetti-filled eggs are used for celebration in Mexico.

Wearing White Ruffles and Lace in Panama

For Panamanians Carnival begins four days before Ash Wednesday. During Carnival in Panama City, the streets are filled with parades, floats, masked people, and confetti. Women and girls traditionally dress in *polleras*, Panama's national costume. The *pollera* is a beautiful costume that originated in the rural areas of Panama's interior. The outfit is composed of two pieces: a shirt called a *camisilla* and a full, gathered skirt with two or three ruffles, called *el pollerón*. The fabric is usually white and is embellished with lace, edging, embroidery, and **appliqué**. Panamanian parades include *comparsas* (Cuban music and dance style) and *tunas* (cheerful groups of musicians and dancers).

Pukllay in Peru

Although Pukllay, representing the spirit of Carnival, is celebrated throughout the Andes Mountains with music and dancing, in the highlands (such as in Northern Argentina) the festival differs from the same celebration at lower altitudes. In some parts of Peru the dances and rituals have a decidedly romantic slant. Couples from Chillihuani, Peru, dance at Tusuna Q'asa Pata, which means "the high place between the mountains." This is the first in a series of ceremonies leading to marriage. The bride and groom can marry in a traditional wedding, known as *rimanakuy*, any time after Pukllay. During *rimanukuy*, the parents of the young couple meet and discuss with them what it means to be married. This is a legal and binding marriage, undertaken in the presence of the parents and the Andean gods. Sometimes the couple decides to follow it up with a Catholic marriage (*casarakuy* in Quechua).

Carnival Traditions in Puerto Rico

Many costumes and masks now common throughout the Caribbean originated in Ponce, the second-largest city in Puerto Rico. It was in Ponce that residents celebrated the first Caribbean Carnival, with music, masks, and costumes, in the 1700s. The papier-mâché masks are painted in bright colors to look as frightening as possible, with bulging eyes, long twisted horns, and fang-toothed grins. These characters are called *vejigantes* and they represent the battle between good and evil.

The *vejigantes* are associated with different holidays in different towns. For example, in Loíza (a small town on Puerto Rico's northeastern coast) *vejigantes* are part of a July celebration honoring Santiago (Saint James), the patron saint of Spain. The *vejigantes* also show up in Hatillo (a municipality on the north coast) during a December holiday commemorating the Death of the Innocents. Although *vejigantes* are part of each town's holiday, the masks produced by that town's artists are distinctive. All the masks are scary and colorful, but those of Loíza are carved from wood and coconut husks, whereas the ones from Hatillo incorporate metal strings, in imitation of soldiers' armor.

The *vejigante's* costume is usually made from a variety of cloth scraps and features bat-like sleeves that make the character look bigger and more menacing. The *vejigantes* roam the streets and tease people, especially children. Like Diablo Cojuelo of the Dominican Republic's Carnival, they each carry an inflated cow bladder–today it is usually a plastic substitute or a balloon–and swat people with it. The little children are scared of these characters, but the older children are eager to join them. They can become *vejigantes* as soon as their families give them permission. Costumes are popular for everyone, however. In Ponce these are typically one-piece overalls in red and yellow (the colors of the Spanish flag) or in red and black (the colors of the city of Ponce).

▲ A costumed troupe parades to calypso music in Saint Lucia, during Mardi Gras, one of this Caribbean island's biggest Carnival events.

Christmastime Carnival in Saint Kitts and Nevis

Carnival is the biggest event of the year in Saint Kitts and Nevis—a nation of volcanic islands with a long history of British rule and struggles for independence. Unlike the traditional Carnivals held in February in most countries,

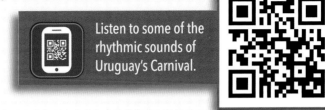

Listen to some of the rhythmic sounds of Uruguay's Carnival.

this Carnival begins on Christmas Eve, December 24, and ends in early January, much like the celebration of the Twelve Days of Christmas. Carnival in Saint Kitts and Nevis is a time for beauty pageants, calypso poetry contests, parades, and street dancing. People participate in masquerades and wear brightly colored costumes. The final day of Carnival ends with the Carnival Last Lap, a parade of costumed bands and street dancing.

Vincy Mas in Saint Vincent and the Grenadines

Originally a pre-Lenten observance, the Carnival in Saint Vincent and the Grenadines was moved to summer (late June and early July) so it would not conflict with other Carnivals in the Caribbean region. The celebration, also known as *Vincy Mas*, is the biggest event in the country. On the opening day of Vincy Mas, revelers disguised as devils paint their faces and bodies with mud and roam the streets until the early morning hours. For about the next 10 days, street parties, beauty pageants, and parades take

BLACK DEVIL COSTUMES IN VENEZUELA

In the region of El Callao, Venezuela, people wear red and black devil costumes with horns. The black devils are the most dangerous since they paint themselves black and splash black paint on anyone who comes near them.

place, mainly in Kingstown, the capital. People dress up in colorful clothes and compete for the titles of best calypso poet and best soca, jazz, and reggae musicians. The main attraction of Vincy Mas is the Miss Carnival beauty pageant.

▲ A man sings during Carnival celebrations in Montevideo, Uruguay.

■ African-Inspired Music and Dance in Uruguay

During Carnival, the southern South American country of Uruguay transforms itself into one big party. In the celebrations two weeks prior to the start of Lent, people wear masks and colorful costumes and play pranks on each other. Water fights are especially popular. One of the high points of the festival is the *candombe*, a popular dance that originated with the enslaved Africans who were brought to work in Uruguay. With 50 to 100 drummers and dancers in each group, the *candombe* performances are the major highlights of Carnival.

■ Burning Judas in Venezuela

Carnival festivities in Venezuela are marked by dances, costumes, songs, bullfights, and pageants, as well as the staging of plays such as *La Quemada de Judas* ("The Burning of Judas"). This play features an effigy, or representation, of Judas, the disciple who betrayed Jesus by identifying him to Roman soldiers, who arrested and killed him. At the conclusion of the play, the effigy of Judas is thrown onto a bonfire and burned to ashes.

The biggest Carnival celebration takes place in the region of El Callao, the largest port city in Peru (located west of Lima, the country's capital), where revelers dress in colorful costumes, wear masks and costumes of cartoon characters and superheroes, and march to calypso music. Some costumes are inspired by traditional attire, most notably that of the Madamas, who dress themselves in the style of women from Guadeloupe and Martinique, complete with traditional headscarves.

 TEXT-DEPENDENT QUESTIONS

1: Why does the nation of Antigua and Barbuda hold Carnival during summer?

2: What agricultural event marks the beginning of Carnival in Argentina?

3: What was the first song written specifically for Carnival in Brazil?

4: What is another name of Carnival in Saint Vincent and the Grenadines?

 RESEARCH PROJECTS

1: Research the Sambadrome in Brazil. Gather information about its history, architecture, location, and the various events it has hosted. Write a brief report giving an overview of all this information.

2: Find a famous calypsonian and research his or her biography, including the place they were born, how they became involved in calypso, and some of their notable accomplishments. Write a brief summary of their life and their contributions to the calypso art form.

Celebrating in North America

Carnival has long been a tradition in New Orleans, Louisiana, and Mobile, Alabama, but more recently, with the holiday gaining in popularity around the world, other North American cities have joined in the fun. Some of the larger celebrations occur in the Canadian province of Québec, and in Miami, Florida; Saint Paul, Minnesota; and San Francisco, California. There is also a Carnival celebration in New York City; however, it is not related to the Christian holiday of Lent. For that reason, it does not take place before the Lenten season, but rather during Labor Day weekend.

WORDS TO UNDERSTAND

Cajun: The culture or people living in the Louisiana area who descended from the French Canadians of Acadia (around what is now Nova Scotia) and settled in the area around New Orleans.

Gumbo: In Cajun cooking, a thick soup typically made with okra, meat or seafood, vegetables, and spices.

Jambalaya: A traditional Creole dish from the New Orleans area, consisting of rice cooked with chicken, sausage, ham, or shellfish, many vegetables, and different spices.

Levee: A ridge of earth designed to keep out floodwaters.

◀ A woman dressed in her Fat Tuesday costume in New Orleans, Louisiana.

The First Mardi Gras in North America: Mobile, Alabama

It is a point of pride in Mobile, Alabama, that this city held the first Mardi Gras celebration in North America in 1703, which was before the city of New Orleans was even established. Furthermore, the first Mardi Gras krewe in New Orleans was founded by men from Mobile. The Mardi Gras krewes, or societies, are the driving force behind the Mardi Gras festivities. It is the members of these krewes who all year long plan the parade floats, costumes, and balls that make Mardi Gras such a colorful exciting event. The krewes keep their plans secret as they compete against one another each year for the best costumes and floats.

MYSTICS OF CHILDREN

In 1965, a Mobile resident helped a group of children decorate a small red wagon, which they then paraded through their neighborhood. This was the basis for the founding of the Mystics of Children, a group that sponsors floats decorated by children.

The first secret Mardi Gras society, Masque de la Mobile, was formed in 1704. While similar societies in New Orleans are called krewes, these groups in Mobile came to be called *mystic societies*. In 1711, people celebrated Mardi Gras by singing, feasting, dancing, and pushing a papier-mâché bull down a main street. Some believe this to be the first Carnival parade in North America.

According to Mobilian Mardi Gras legend, the story begins on New Year's Eve, 1829. A newcomer from Pennsylvania Dutch country named Michael Krafft went out to dinner with some friends. After dinner, the men did not want the night to end, so they came up with a silly idea that would later prove to be very significant. Upon passing a display at a local hardware store, the men "borrowed" several items, including rakes, hoes, and cowbells, and paraded through the streets making as much noise as possible. This impromptu procession awoke the mayor, who is said to have later challenged the men to plan and stage a formal parade the following New Year's Eve. Krafft and his friends responded by forming the Cowbellion de Rakin Society. Their festivities continued to take place on New Year's Eve for some years but eventually evolved into today's Mardi Gras celebration.

The Civil War (1861–65) forced the suspension of Mardi Gras as the city of Mobile suffered under a federal occupation by the Union Army, which blockaded all shipping activity in and out of Mobile Bay. This blockade continued even after the war ended. In 1866, while the city was still under occupation, a store clerk named Joseph Cain decided to revive the tradition of the costumed Mardi Gras parade in the hope that it would encourage and energize the people of Mobile.

Cain dressed up as a Chickasaw Indian, called himself Chief Slacabamorinico, and rode through the streets of the city on a coal wagon with a few other costumed revelers. The makeshift costume was not chosen randomly: The Chickasaw tribe had never surrendered to the Union forces during the Civil War. Not only did Cain restore the tradition of the Mardi Gras parade but he also slyly resisted the Union troops—and got away with it.

Today, Mobile's Mardi Gras is widely known for its focus on families and children, who are eager participants in the parades and festivities. As in the New Orleans Mardi Gras, the people riding floats in parades throw goodies to the excited spectators—colorful plastic beads, doubloon coins, candy, and Moon Pies—cookie sandwiches filled with marshmallow that are popular in the Deep South.

■ Mardi Gras in Louisiana

Nearly a million tourists from around the world descend on New Orleans, Louisiana, each year for the celebration of Mardi Gras. While dwarfed by the excesses of the New Orleans festivities, southern Louisiana cities such as Lafayette and Houma also have Carnival celebrations, featuring all the parades, dances, and food and drink of their international counterparts.

JOE CAIN DAY

Joseph Cain's revival of Mardi Gras is commemorated every year on the Sunday before Mardi Gras, now known as Joe Cain Day. This day is dedicated to the people, and all are invited to participate in the procession with their own homemade floats and costumes.

MOON PIES AND CRACKER JACK

Before the Moon Pies were introduced, riders on floats threw boxes of Cracker Jack (caramel-covered popcorn and peanuts) to spectators. When Moon Pies became popular, people realized their plastic packaging had no edges and was much safer than Cracker Jack. To prevent injuries to parade-goers, it is now illegal to throw Cracker Jack boxes.

AN AMERICAN CITY WITH DEEP FRENCH ROOTS: NEW ORLEANS

New Orleans was founded by the French in 1718. In the early years, the city's residents included French settlers, French Canadians, and enslaved Native Americans. African slaves transplanted to the Caribbean and North America during the colonial period also contributed to the development of the region, including the way Carnival is celebrated. New Orleans remained under the French flag until the territory of Louisiana was secretly ceded to Spain in 1763. Under Spanish rule, New Orleans grew and became a busy trading center. In 1800, the colony of Louisiana was returned to France (again secretly), and in 1803 France's emperor, Napoleon I, sold the entire Mississippi valley to the United States for about $15 million. One of the greatest real estate bargains in history, the sale became known as the Louisiana Purchase. Louisiana became a U.S. State in 1812.

As a result of this history, New Orleans has a diverse cultural heritage. In addition to the mix of French, Spanish, African, and Native American cultures, the area surrounding New Orleans is home to the **Cajun** people, who have a strong and distinct culture. The term *Cajun* comes from the word "Acadian," which refers to the French Canadian people from the colony known as Acadia in (and around) modern-day Nova Scotia, Canada. In 1754 the British forced the Acadians to leave Canada because they refused to declare loyalty to the Protestant English king and give up their Catholic religion. Between 4,000 and 5,000 Acadians were driven out of their homeland, and in 1764 and 1765 more than 200 of them landed in Louisiana. (The story forms the basis of an early classic of American literature, Henry Wadsworth Longfellow's *Evangeline: A Tale of Arcadie*, first published in 1847.)

During the 20 years that followed, about 3,000 more Acadians arrived. Most of them settled in rural areas west of New Orleans and throughout southern and southwestern Louisiana. They did the work that no one else would do, such as clearing land that others considered worthless. Since they were poor and illiterate, and arrived with a foreign language and culture, they did not fit in well with the larger community. The Acadians were rejected, even by other French speakers in Louisiana, because they spoke an unfamiliar French dialect. Consequently, the Acadians continued to maintain close family ties and tended to marry other Acadians. Over time, they became known as Cajuns. Even as they became more integrated in society, the Cajuns managed to preserve their rich culture. Today, many descendants of the Acadians still speak a dialect that combines French with words and expressions borrowed from the languages of the people who have surrounded them in the New Orleans area, including Spanish, German, English, and Native American languages.

New Orleans is also home to people of Irish, German, and Italian descent who immigrated to the area around the 1840s. One of the strongest and most distinct cultural traditions in New Orleans is the African-American tradition. Enslaved Africans were among the first settlers in the city, and their descendants have shaped every aspect of life there, from politics to business to food to the arts. In fact, New Orleans is world famous as the birthplace of jazz, a musical form developed in the African-American community in the early 20th century.

THE ORIGINS OF MARDI GRAS IN NEW ORLEANS

Historical documentation of the early period of Mardi Gras history is scarce, but most historians believe that pre-Lenten celebrations were quite common in New Orleans by the late 1700s. The majority of these celebrations most likely took the form of masked balls. The first documented Mardi Gras parade made its way through New Orleans in 1837. During the two decades following this event, the atmosphere of the parades became progressively more violent and unruly, and many people called for a ban on the parades and celebrations.

In 1857, in response to the public outcry, a small group of men from Mobile, Alabama established the first Carnival krewe, an organization dedicated to the celebration of Carnival. These men had been leading New Year's Eve parades in Mobile since 1831. They proposed a plan to establish a safer, more organized Mardi Gras parade. Their proposal was approved by local leaders, and they gave themselves the name of the Mystick Krewe of Comus. The name, which contains some intentional misspellings, was inspired by John Milton's poem "A Mask Presented at Ludlow Castle," which makes reference to "Comus with his crew." Comus, the Greek god of revelry, was

▲ The Bacchagator float turns onto Saint Charles Avenue during the Krewe of Bacchus Mardi Gras parade in New Orleans.

▲ The year's Rex, King of Carnival, leads the way through the crowd in New Orleans on Mardi Gras.

a follower of Dionysus, the Greek god of wine. Although the members of Comus were trying to clean up Carnival, they clearly wanted to maintain an atmosphere of festive celebration and fun. The Mystick Krewe of Comus paraded through New Orleans for the first time during the Mardi Gras celebration of 1857. In addition to the parade, which featured mule-drawn floats, costumed riders, and torch carriers to light the way, there was also a grand costume ball. The Comus Krewe established several traditions that would be carried on by later krewes, including mythological krewe names and themes for parades and balls.

A PARADE FIT FOR A KING

In 1872 a group of New Orleans businessmen learned that the grand duke of Russia, Alexis Romanov, was planning to travel to the city during Carnival. These men decided to honor the grand duke with a special parade, which they called *Rex*, from the Latin word for "king." Likewise, they named their newly formed society the Krewe of Rex and took the colors of the Romanov family:

purple, green, and gold. These colors, which represent justice, faith, and power, respectively, are now the official colors of the Mardi Gras celebration. The official song of Mardi Gras, "If Ever I Cease to Love," also originated with the Krewe of Rex in 1872. Having heard that this was the grand duke's favorite song, they hired a band to play it during the first Rex parade.

According to Mardi Gras lore, that year the Krewe of Rex demanded that the city be closed and the keys to the city be given to a costumed character called Rex, the King of Carnival. Since that year, the character of Rex has been the symbolic King of Carnival. Today, the Rex parade is one of the highlights of Mardi Gras, held on the final day of Carnival.

FATTENED BULL

One of the most popular floats from the Rex parade features the *boeuf gras*, or fattened bull, the traditional symbol of the last meat eaten before the beginning of the Lenten fast. Today this bull is represented on the float in the form of a huge papier-mâché figure.

THE MODERN MARDI GRAS CELEBRATION

Every year, on the Feast of the Three Kings (January 6), a group of revelers known as the Phunny Phorty Phellows marks the beginning of the Carnival season with a festive ride through New Orleans on a streetcar. Then, about two weeks before Mardi Gras, the parades begin. Today, there are more than two dozen Carnival krewes, each with its own traditions.

Over the years, local government has implemented laws to preserve the authentic nature of the Mardi Gras celebration, while also ensuring that the event includes the many diverse groups of people who live in New Orleans and have shared equally in its history. One such law, implemented in 1992, requires all parade krewes to be racially integrated. Another law prevents corporate sponsorship in the Mardi Gras parades.

During Mardi Gras parades, brightly colored beads, plastic coins, and candy fly through the air in a tradition much loved by parade-goers–especially the children. Krewe members riding on floats toss the trinkets in keeping with a custom thought to have begun in 1871 when a reveler dressed as Santa Claus handed out gifts from his float. Today, the most prized collectibles are those that feature the krewe's name and emblem and a representation of the parade's theme. Spectators shout, "Throw me something!" to get the attention of trinket-tossers on passing floats.

▲ A masked rider throws beads during the Krewe of Iris Mardi Gras parade in New Orleans.

THE MUSIC OF RIO

Children who like music and dancing will love the Rio Carnival celebration put on a few days before Mardi Gras by a samba music and dance troupe based in New Orleans. Here kids can learn all about the Carnival traditions in Rio, and even play their own samba music.

Mardi Gras also offers many events planned especially for children. These events are organized by different groups, including churches, the city government, and the Carnival krewes. Children engage in arts and crafts, listen to stories, attend special costume balls and parades, and bake, and decorate. They can learn how to make their own floats, paint their faces, create masks, or twist balloons into animal shapes. Musical groups perform different types of music from all over the world, such as flamenco music from Spain and samba music from Brazil. They also play musical styles that originated in and around New Orleans itself, such as jazz and zydeco.

THE MARDI GRAS INDIANS

Like New Orleans society, Mardi Gras celebrations have not always been open to everyone. For a long time, the parades, the masked balls, even the krewes themselves, were for invited guests only. Later, when these events were opened to the public, they remained inaccessible to the lower classes, often because they were just too expensive.

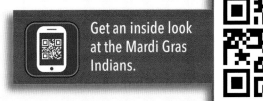 

Get an inside look at the Mardi Gras Indians.

One group in particular was often left out: African Americans. But while the exclusive, white Mardi Gras parades rolled on without them, African Americans created their own traditions of music, dance, and parading, and their own secret societies, known as the Mardi Gras Indians. Beginning as early as the mid-18th century, groups of African Americans in poor neighborhoods of New Orleans prepared elaborate costumes that resembled ceremonial Native American dress and performed dances and chants reminiscent of traditional Native American celebrations.

Why the African Americans chose to dress as American Indians is not clear. Some people believe the costumes and celebrations were inspired by traveling Wild West shows from the late 1800s, but this theory does not mesh with records from 1746 that mention African Americans dressing as Indians. Others say African Americans donned costumes to sneak into the French Quarter and join the celebration during times of segregation. They may have been helped by Native Americans, in solidarity against the Europeans. It is also possible that African Americans adopted Indian dress to pay tribute to the Native Americans who had helped blacks escape slavery.

For more than 200 years the various groups of Mardi Gras Indians, known as *tribes*, have engaged in intense competition. In the past, this competition sometimes led to real conflicts and confrontations. In 1987, the New Orleans Mardi Gras Indian Council was

ORIGINS OF ZYDECO

In southwest Louisiana during the 16th century, the young people of the Atakapa tribe enjoyed a lively social dance that had a strong rhythm. The dance was named *shi ishol*, because the Atakapa word for dance is *shi* (rhymes with "sky"), and "youths" is *ishol*. When the Spaniards discovered the Atakapa in 1528, they translated *shi ishol* as *zy ikol*. Four hundred years later, the descendants of the Atakapas and the Africans are still enjoying lively social dancing with a strong beat, but today they call it *zydeco*.

formed in order to oversee the celebration and preserve the culture of the Mardi Gras Indians. Then, in 1992, the Big Chiefs of all the main tribes gathered together in celebration as a sign of unity. These measures have helped transform the celebrations into peaceful events. In the past, tribes passing on the street might have started to fight; now they often start an impromptu competition to see which tribe has the best chant, song, dance, and costumes.

Extensive preparation goes into each costume, with tribe members spending sometimes thousands of dollars buying sequins, glass beads, ostrich feathers, dye, and other materials. In some tribes only the chief sews the costumes, whereas in others all the members sew as a community activity. Either way, the work usually takes the entire year. The finished products are extraordinary—especially the long colorful feathers extending all around the costume wearer and high over his or her head. The front of the costume may bear a painted scene of historical significance for African Americans or Native Americans. The costumes are always unique, and many are now preserved in museums and recognized as outstanding examples of folk art. On Mardi Gras, the tribes display their extraordinary costumes in parades that wind through the city's African American neighborhoods.

KING CAKES A-PLENTY

New Orleans is known around the world for delicious food from **jambalaya** (a dish traditionally made in one pot, with meats, vegetables, and rice) to **gumbo** (a stew made with chicken, seafood, greens, and okra) to beignets (fritters that are much like doughnuts). But at Mardi Gras, the king cake reigns supreme. Made from dough that is rolled into the shape of a crown and sometimes braided, the cake is often topped with sugary treats and decorated with the vibrant purple, green, and gold of Mardi Gras. Some cakes are also filled with rich custard. Thousands of king cakes are baked and sold each Carnival season, beginning on January 6. The tradition of baking these pastries was brought over by the original French settlers, and it is still practiced in Europe and many other Christian areas of the world in addition to New Orleans. The name of the cake comes from the holiday for which it is made, the

THE BABY IN THE CAKE

Hidden inside each king cake is a bean or a small plastic baby (representing the baby Jesus). When the bean or baby turns up in someone's piece, that person may be expected to throw a party for everyone present—or to provide the next king cake. If someone is lucky enough to find the baby at one of several elegant balls, he or she may be named king or queen of that krewe's parade!

◀ A large king cake, traditional harbinger of Mardi Gras, iced in Carnival colors, is shown at a Louisiana bakery. Mardi Gras beads surround the cake, and a handful of doubloons lie in its center.

Feast of the Three Kings. This holiday, which celebrates the visit of the Three Wise Men to the baby Jesus, is also called the Feast of the Epiphany. While this type of cake is only made for the Day of the Three Kings in some places, it is eaten all throughout the Carnival season in New Orleans.

MARDI GRAS GUMBO

Going to New Orleans and not eating gumbo would be a bit like visiting Italy and not eating pasta. Gumbo is a typical Southern dish that probably has as many variations as there are cooks. It begins with a base of water and roux, a thickening agent usually made of white flour and butter, fat, or vegetable oil. The cook adds vegetables and seafood or meat, such as chicken, sausage, or rabbit. The gumbo is seasoned with garlic, parsley, salt, black pepper, and spicy cayenne pepper. As the mixture is heated, it thickens. The finished gumbo is served over rice and eaten with delight.

Cajuns and Creoles, Americans descended from colonial French or Spanish Louisianans, part ways on how to thicken gumbo. Cajun gumbo usually uses okra, a vegetable popular in the American South as well as the Middle East, India, the Caribbean, and Africa. In place of okra, Creole gumbo uses filé (a ground spice mixture of thyme and sassafras oil) as a thickener and includes tomatoes. In the past Cajun gumbo was made up of meats, such as chicken, sausage, and fresh game, whereas Creole gumbo focused on seafood. Some cooks feel that putting both okra and filé in a gumbo would be as unthinkable as putting mustard on ice cream. Other cooks believe the only important rule is that gumbo should taste good.

THE EFFECT OF HURRICANE KATRINA ON NEW ORLEANS AND MARDI GRAS

On August 25, 2005, Hurricane Katrina hit the Louisiana coast. Perhaps the worst natural disaster in American history, the storm overwhelmed the **levees**, which are sloped, earthen embankments meant to protect the city from flooding. Since the city has an elevation as low as 5 to 10 feet below sea level in some places, the floodwaters proved too powerful to stop. Over the next two days, nearly 80 percent of New Orleans was flooded. Many New Orleans residents had evacuated ahead of the storm. But thousands of people had stayed behind, and in the days following the hurricane, they struggled to escape their houses and reach flood shelters. Though many did make their way to safety, more than 2,000 people died or were declared missing, and large areas of the city were destroyed.

Since the storm, New Orleanians and volunteers from across the country have joined in an extraordinary effort to repair and reconstruct the historic city. Just months after the hurricane, the people of New Orleans demonstrated their strength and resilience by dressing up, singing, dancing, parading, eating, drinking, and celebrating Mardi Gras, as they have every year since then.

THE GUMBO MIX

Gumbo is so popular that books have been written about it, and not just cookbooks. Some communities hold annual gumbo cook-offs, and musicians record albums with names like "Lousiana Gumbo" or "Christmas Gumbo." There is even a magazine called *Gumbo Teen*, which is written by teenagers for teenaged readers. Like New Orleans itself, gumbo is a mixture of flavors from different cultures. The roux thickener comes from classic French cooking, the filé spice mixture probably originated with the Choctaw Indians, and okra was brought to the South by the slave trade. It is a dish that crosses all social barriers and is very forgiving—the cook can use what is available and measurements do not have to be exact. *The Creole Cookery Book* (Christian Woman's Exchange, 1885) calls making gumbo an "occult science ... that should be allowed its proper place in the gastronomical world."

MARDI GRAS IN CAJUN COUNTRY

Although New Orleans is famous for its Carnival festivities, Mardi Gras celebrations are held throughout communities of southern Louisiana. Unique customs have developed in rural areas that distinguish the festivities from those in New Orleans. In a tradition called the *courir* (French for "run"), which began in French regions of Louisiana sometime in the 19th century, costumed participants go from house to house asking for food or money to contribute to a communal meal that evening. The meal, which will be cooked in a central area for all to enjoy, is usually gumbo, accompanied by sweet potatoes, potato salad, and rice.

The participants, or runners, are called Mardi Gras, and today they travel either on foot, on horseback, or on flatbed trailers towed by tractors or trucks. They are led by a capitaine, who directs their march. Upon arrival at a house, the capitaine will request permission to come onto the property. Once permission is granted, the Mardi Gras run toward the house, singing, dancing, and asking for a donation for gumbo. At times, the Mardi Gras may demand more from a homeowner if they believe he or she has not given enough. The request is made with an extravagant performance of song, dance, and foolishness designed to entertain the homeowner. Following a donation, the Mardi Gras may thank the donor with different ceremonies, such as gathering around the contributor in a circle and hoisting him or her up in the air, just as sports teams lift a member who made a winning play. In the afternoon the Mardi Gras return to town with their donated food items and parade down the main street to the place where the communal meal will be cooked.

THROWING THE CHICKEN

If the Mardi Gras come calling at a home that has a live chicken to donate, the homeowner may throw the chicken into an open field, forcing the runners to chase it all about until they are able to catch it.

CAJUN MUSIC

Traditional Cajun music incorporates a combination of musical styles from different peoples who have lived in Louisiana since the Cajun people settled there, such as French, Spanish, Germans, and black Creoles. Many Cajun instruments were borrowed from these peoples–including the accordion, borrowed from the Germans, and the guitar from the Spanish. Zydeco music, which is a popularized, electrified, and lively adaptation of Cajun music, is played all around Louisiana during the Mardi Gras season.

ICE PALACES IN SAINT PAUL

Over its long history, the Saint Paul Carnival has commissioned the construction of 36 ice palaces. The first, built in 1886, was 106 feet high.

The Mardi Gras observances in these southern Louisiana communities have great significance. The bright color, energetic music, and celebration liven up the drab winter season, anticipating the blossoming of spring that will soon arrive. The traditions of the *courir* and the communal meal also serve to reinforce bonds within the community. Those who have more are expected to share with those who have less, and the traveling Mardi Gras see that they do so. Everyone is expected to contribute somehow to the celebration, and, everyone is invited to enjoy the communal gumbo prepared in the evening.

◼ Saint Paul, Minnesota

In response to a steady population increase and the industrial boom in the late 19th century, business leaders of Saint Paul organized the first Winter Carnival in 1886. The event took place over the first two weeks of February and featured parades and many winter sports such as skiing, toboggan sledding, and snowshoeing.

Today's Winter Carnival is designed for families and offers programs and workshops for children on science and weather, foreign languages, music, magic, mosaic making, and traditional Chinese dance. Children can also compete for prizes in ice carving, snow sculpting, coloring, and jigsaw puzzles. Adults can take part in more traditional activities, such as golfing or racing.

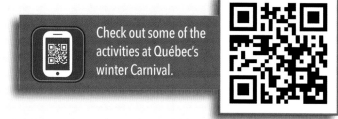

Check out some of the activities at Québec's winter Carnival.

◼ Carnival de Québec

The Carnival of Québec in Canada is also about enjoying the pleasures of winter. Québec's winter carnival began in 1894, although it was not celebrated during World War I (1914–18) and World War II (1939–45), or around the time of the Great Depression (which began in 1929). Between

▲ A man puts the finishing touch on a tower as a crew completes the building of the Québec winter Carnival ice castle in Québec City, Canada.

1945 and 1955 the Carnival was held inconsistently and seemed to have lost its focus. The modern form of the celebration was launched in 1955 and has continued yearly since. In 1955 a mascot for the Carnival was introduced: Bonhomme, a tall, laughing snowman dressed like a French voyager, or explorer, who represents Québec's French past.

Québec's is thought to be the largest winter Carnival in the world. The Carnival begins on the last Friday in January and runs for 17 days. Since 1955 many more events have been added, so that there are now activities for all ages and interests. The planners try to achieve a balance between tradition and modern times, between commemorating their region's history and simply having fun. There is a broad range of activities, such as eating a flapjack (pancake) breakfast, attending music concerts or grand balls, painting seminars, and even watching a Chinese martial arts demonstration. For those who like to be active and do not mind the cold, the celebration offers outdoor activities such as ice sculpting, snow sculpting, winter sports, free lessons in alpine skiing for children, and dogsled races through the streets of the city. There is also the famous canoe race

▲ Teams racing in the annual Québec winter Carnival ice canoe race in Québec City, Canada.

across the Saint Lawrence River. Naturally, since most bodies of water are frozen, the canoes must navigate over ice and snow. Celebrants traditionally wear red hats and fringed belts reminiscent of the kind worn by Native Americans of the region.

 TEXT-DEPENDENT QUESTIONS

1: What is the official song of Mardi Gras in New Orleans?

2: Where does the Mardi Gras king cake get its name?

3: What were the effects of Hurricane Katrina on the city of New Orleans?

4: In what year did Québec's winter Carnival begin?

RESEARCH PROJECTS

1: Research one of the Native American tribes indigenous to Lousiana, such as the Choctaw, Chitimacha, or the Houma. Discover facts about their history, their contributions to local culture, and any involvement they might have in Mardi Gras. Write a summary of your findings.

2: Find another winter festival similar to Québec's winter Carnival. Examples include the Sapporo Snow Festival in Japan, Winterlude in Ottawa, Canada, and the Momentum Ski Festival in Switzerland. Research the festival's history, events, attendance, and other facts. Prepare a tourist brochure introducing potential visitors to the festival.

▲ A marching band processes down Bourbon Street during Mardi Gras festivities in the French Quarter of New Orleans.

Series Glossary

ancestors The direct family members of one who is deceased

aristocrat A member of a high social class, the nobility, or the ruling class

atonement The act of making up for sins so that they may be forgiven

ayatollah A major religious leader, scholar, and teacher in Shii Islam; the religious leader of Iran

colonial era A period of time between the 17th to 19th century when many countries of the Americas and Africa were colonized by Europeans.

colonize To travel to and settle in a foreign land that has already been settled by groups of people. To colonize can mean to take control of the indigenous groups already in the area or to wield power over them in order to control their human and physical resources.

commemorate To honor the memory of a person or event

commercialization The act of reorganizing or reworking something in order to extract profit from it

descendant One who comes from a specific ancestor

Eastern Orthodox Church The group of Christian churches that includes the Greek Orthodox, Russian Orthodox, and several other churches led by patriarchs in Istanbul (Constantinople), Jerusalem, Antioch, and Alexandria.

effigy A representation of someone or something, often used for mockery

equinox Either of the two times during each year when night and day are approximately the same length of time. The spring equinox typically falls around March 21 and the autumnal equinox around September 23.

fast To abstain from eating for a set period of time, or to eat at only prescribed times of the day as directed by religious custom or law.

feast day A day when a religious celebration occurs and an intricate feast is prepared and eaten.

firsthand From the original source; experienced in person

Five Pillars of Islam The five duties Muslims must observe: declaring that there is only one God and Muhammad is his prophet, praying five times a day, giving to charity, fasting during Ramadan, and making a pilgrimage to Mecca

foundation myth A story that describes the foundation of a nation in a way that inspires its people

Gregorian calendar The calendar in use through most of the world

hedonism The belief that pleasure is the sole good in life

Hindu A follower of Hinduism, the dominant religion of India

imam A leader; a scholar of Islam; the head of a mosque

indigenous Originating in or native to a specific region; often refers to living things such as people, animals, and plants

Islam The religious faith of Muslims. Muslims believe that Allah is the only God, and Muhammad was his prophet

Judaism A religion that developed among the ancient Hebrews. Followers of Judaism believe in one God and follow specific laws written in the Torah and the Talmud, and revealed to them by Moses.

Julian calendar Is named after Julius Caesar, a military leader and dictator of ancient Rome, who introduced it in 46 B.C.E. The Julian calendar has 365 days divided into 12 months, and begins on January 1. An extra day, or leap day, is added every four years (February 29) so that the years will average out to 365.242, which is quite close to the actual 365.242199 days of Earth's orbit.

lower realm In the Asian tradition, the place where the souls end up if their actions on Earth were not good

lunar Related to the Moon

martyr A person who willingly undergoes pain or death because of a strong belief or principle

masquerade A party to which people wear masks, and sometimes costumes or disguises

millennium 1,000 years

monarch A king or queen; a ruler who inherits the throne from a parent or other relative

monotheism The belief in the supremacy of one god (and not many) that began with Judaism more than 4,000 years ago and also includes the major religions of Islam and Christianity.

mosque An Islamic house of worship

mourning The expression of sorrow for the loss of a loved one, typically involving

movable feast A religious feast day that occurs on a different day every year

Muhammad The prophet to whom God revealed the Quran, considered the final prophet of Islam

mullah A clergyman who is an expert on the Quran and Islamic religious matters

Muslim A person who follows the Islamic religion

New Testament The books of the Bible that were written after the birth of Christ

New World A term used to describe the Americas from the point of view of the Western Europeans (especially those from France, England, Portugal, and Spain) who colonized and settled what is today North and South America.

offering Donation of food or money given in the name of a deity or God

Old Testament The Christian term for the Hebrew Scriptures of the Bible, written before the birth of Christ

oral tradition Stories told aloud, rather than written, as a way to pass down history

pagan Originally, someone in ancient Europe who lived in the countryside; a person or group that does not believe in one god, but often believes in many gods that are closely connected to nature and the natural world

pageantry Spectacle, elaborate display

parody Imitation of something, exaggerated for comic effect—for example, a parody of science fiction movies.

patria Fatherland; nation; homeland

peasant People who farm land that usually belongs to someone else, such as a landowner

penance The repentance of sins, including confessing, expressing regret for having committed them, and doing something to earn forgiveness

piety A strong belief in and correspondingly fervent practice of religion

pilgrimage A journey undertaken to a specific destination, often for religious purposes

prank A mischievous or humorous trick

pre-Columbian Of or relating to the period before Christopher Columbus arrived in the Americas

procession A group of people moving together in the same direction, especially in a type of celebration

prophecy A prediction about a future event

prophet An individual who acts as the interpreter or conveyer of the will of God and spreads the word to the followers or possible followers of a religion. A prophet can also be a stirring leader or teacher of a religious group. Capitalized it refers to Muhammad.

Protestant A member of a Christian denomination that does not follow the rule of the pope in Rome and is not one of the Eastern Orthodox Churches. Protestant denominations include Anglicans (Episcopalians), Lutherans, Presbyterians, Methodists, Baptists, and many others.

Quran The holy book of Islam

rabbi A Jew who is ordained to lead a Jewish congregation; rabbis are traditionally teachers of Judaism.

reincarnation The belief in some religions that after a person or animal dies, his or her soul will be reborn in another person or animal; it literally means, "to be made flesh again." Many Indian religions such as Hinduism, Sikhism, and Jainism, believe in reincarnation.

repentance To express regret and ask forgiveness for doing something wrong or hurtful.

requiem A Mass for the souls of the dead, especially in the Catholic Church

revel To celebrate in a joyful manner; to take extreme pleasure

ritual A specific action or ceremony typically of religious significance

sacred Connected with God or religious purposes and deemed worthy of veneration and worship

sacrifice Something given up or offered in the name of God, a deity or an ancestor.

shaman A spiritual guide who a community believes has unique powers to tell the future and to heal the sick. Shamans can mediate or cooperate with spirits for a community's advantage. Cultures that practice shamanism are found all over the world still today.

Shia A Muslim sect that believes that Ali, Muhammad's son-in-law, should have succeeded Muhammad as the caliph of Islam; a common sect in Iran but worldwide encompassing only about 15 percent of Muslims

solar calendar A calendar that is based on the time it takes Earth to orbit once around the Sun

solar Related to the Sun

solilunar Relating to both the Sun and Moon

solstice Day of the year when the hours of daylight are longest or shortest. The solstices mark the changing of the seasons–when summer begins in the Northern Hemisphere (about June 22) and winter begins in the Northern Hemisphere (about December 22).

spiritual Of or relating to the human spirit or soul, or to religious belief

Sunni The largest Islamic sect, including about 85 percent of the world's Muslims

supernatural Existing outside the natural world

Talmud The document that encompasses the body of Jewish law and customs

Torah Jewish scriptures, the first five books of the Hebrew scriptures, which serve as the core of Jewish belief

veneration Honoring a god or a saint with specific practices

vigil A period in which a person stays awake to await some event

Vodou A religion rooted in traditional African beliefs that is practiced mostly in Haiti, although it is very popular in the West Indies as well. Outside of Haiti it is called *Vodun*.

Further Resources

■ Books

New Orleans Carnival Krewes: The History, Spirit & Secrets of Mardi Gras. By Rosary O'Neill. Published in 2014 by The History Press, Mt. Pleasant, S.C. This book looks at the history and traditions of Carnival krewes in New Orleans as well as their influence on contemporary Mardi Gras celebrations.

Rick Steves' European Festivals. By Rick Steves. Published in 2017 by Rick Steves/Avalon Travel, Berkeley, Calif. Join beloved tour guide and television personality Rick Steves on a journey through Europe's most famous festivals, including a stop at the Venice Carnival.

Mardi Gras in Mobile. By L. Craig Roberts. Published in 2015 by The History Press, Mt. Pleasant, S.C. Mobile, Alabama, has a long tradition of Mardi Gras celebrations. Learn more about them in this book authored by a local historian.

Christianity (Major World Religions). By Aaron Bowen. Published in 2017 by Mason Crest, Broomall, Pa. This volume is one in a series exploring the world's major religious traditions. It touches on Christian holy days, festivals, and beliefs pertinent to Carnival, such as Ash Wednesday and Lent.

After the Dance: A Walk Through Carnival in Jacmel, Haiti. By Edwidge Danticat. Published in 2015 by Vintage, New York. Follow Haitian-American novelist Edwidge Danticat as she makes a voyage to her home country for Carnival.

■ Web Sites

Binche Tourist Office. http://www.carnavaldebinche.be/home-eng.html. The Binach Tourist Office Web site offers information about the history of the Binche Carnival.

Brazil's Carnival: How to Celebrate and Survive. http://www.post-gazette.com/life/travel/2008/01/17/Brazil-s-carnival-how-to-celebrate-and-survive/stories/200801170357. This 2008 article from the *Pittsburg Post-Gazette* gives practical recommendations for enjoying the Carnival celebration in Rio de Janeiro from a tourist's perspective.

Carnaval de Québec. https://carnaval.qc.ca/home. The Carnival of Québec is not a traditional Carnival, because it does not take place in the days leading up to Ash Wednesday, the beginning of Lent. Instead, it is a Carnival that celebrates winter and the culture of Québec. Read more about this unique celebration here.

Carnival in Rio Is Dancing to More Commercial Beat. http://www.nytimes.com/2003/02/25/world/carnival-in-rio-is-dancing-to-more-commercial-beat.html. In recent years, the Rio Carnival has become more and more commercialized. The author of this article, from 2003, discusses this inevitable process.

Masked Revels of a Belgian Mardi Gras. http://www.nytimes.com/1989/01/22/travel/masked-revels-of-a-belgian-mardi-gras.html. This article, from the *New York Times* Travel section, describes the Carnival celebration in Binche, Belgium.

The New Orleans Convention and Visitors Bureau. http://www.neworleanscvb.com/. This Web site has a great deal of information about things to do in New Orleans as well as about Mardi Gras.

The Official City of New Orleans Museum Site. http://www.neworleansonline.com/neworleans/arts/museums/. This site is maintained by the New Orleans Tourism Marketing Corporation and includes information on different museums throughout the city.

Official Site of the Belgian Tourist Office for Wallonia. http://www.belgiumtheplaceto.be/. If you are looking to visit the Wallonia region Belgium, this Web site provides ample information on different cultural events, including the Binche Carnival.

The Official Tourism Site of the City of New Orleans. http://www.neworleans online.com/neworleans/mardigras/. This site contains information on tourism in and around the city of New Orleans, including information related to the Mardi Gras celebration.

Portale di Venezia. http://www.carnivalofvenice.com/?lang=en. This Web site briefly describes Carnival in Venice, Italy.

Rio vs. Salvador. https://theculturetrip.com/south-america/brazil/articles/rio-vs-salvador-which-carnival-is-for-you/. If you are interested in learning not just about Carnival in Rio but also in Salvador da Bahia, this Web site offers a quick glimpse at the differences between the two.

Saint Paul Festival & Heritage Foundation. http://www.wintercarnival.com/. Here is a Web site for another non-traditional winter carnival, in Saint Paul, Minnesota.

United Nations Educational, Scientific and Cultural Organization. https://ich.unesco.org/en/RL/carnival-of-binche-00033. This page from the UNESCO Web site contains information about the Proclamation of the Carnival of Binche as a site of Intangible Cultural Heritage.

Index

Picture Credits